THE COOK'S TAROT

"Our Lives are Not in the Laps of the Gods,
But in the Laps of our Cooks."

~lin Yutang

WRITTEN AND ILLUSTRATED BY
Judith Mackay Stirt

4880 Lower Valley Road • Atglen, PA 19310

Copyright © 2014 by Judith Mackay Stirt

Library of Congress Control Number: 2014945575

All rights reserved. No part of this work may be reproduced or used in any form or by any means—graphic, electronic, or mechanical, including photocopying or information storage and retrieval systems—without written permission from the publisher.

The scanning, uploading, and distribution of this book or any part thereof via the Internet or via any other means without the permission of the publisher is illegal and punishable by law. Please purchase only authorized editions and do not participate in or encourage the electronic piracy of copyrighted materials.
"Schiffer," "Schiffer Publishing, Ltd. & Design," and the "Design of pen and inkwell" are registered trademarks of Schiffer Publishing, Ltd.

Type set in Vectis/Univers LT Std

ISBN: 978-0-7643-4620-0
Printed in China

Published by Schiffer Publishing, Ltd.
4880 Lower Valley Road
Atglen, PA 19310
Phone: (610) 593-1777; Fax: (610) 593-2002
E-mail: Info@schifferbooks.com

For our complete selection of fine books on this and related subjects, please visit our website at
www.schifferbooks.com.
You may also write for a free catalog.

This book may be purchased from the publisher.
Please try your bookstore first.

We are always looking for people to
write books on new and related subjects.
If you have an idea for a book, please contact
us at proposals@schifferbooks.com.

Schiffer Publishing's titles are available at special discounts for bulk purchases for sales promotions or premiums. Special editions, including personalized covers, corporate imprints, and excerpts can be created in large quantities for special needs.
For more information, contact the publisher.

Dedicated to Nancy Boyes,

my sister, my best friend,
and original business partner.
This book would not exist
without your emotional support
and technical expertise.
I cannot thank you enough.

Acknowledgments

First of all, I would like to thank my husband, David Hellman, for his support and artistic guidance. He keeps insisting that I learned everything from him, and now I say, for the first time, "Maybe, a little."

My brother Rob, and his wife Kathy, and my nephews Scott and Daniel, are part of the glue that binds me together. My daughter Caroline is the golden thread. (One day she will know this.) And thanks to my mother who held her tongue despite a firm conviction that I was going straight to hell.

Thanks to Allan Wong, who designed the first website free of charge, a debt that I will never be able to repay. Many thanks to Penelope Jane Bahr, a good friend whose support and advice were invaluable. Thank you to Cheryl Lynne Bradley of *Tarot Canada*, who printed my first interview, and Solandia of *Aeclectic Tarot*, who did a review of *Dining with the Major Arcana*, a Tarot-based set of recipe cards published by my sister and myself as an introduction to *The Cook's Tarot*.

I would like to thank Joanne Ash of the Sungoddess Tarot for her support both as a friend and mentor. She has opened my eyes to the depths of Tarot, and both her skill and encouragement have allowed me to believe in myself. Thank you, Jo.

The Internet community has been invaluable in terms of research and support. I would especially like to thank Roxi Sim and Pamela Steele, both Tarot artists with published decks, for their *Tarot Deck Creators* website. I have met so many like-minded souls and have made many professional contacts because of their vision. I have listed my favorite or most influential websites in the Bibliography, as it would take so long to name everyone that has participated in my development. The Academy Awards come to mind as I gather steam.

I would also like to thank all my colleagues at work. The Emergency Departments of The Cowichan District Hospital and Nanaimo Regional General Hospital are blessed to have such caring individuals as part of their workforce. I have never met such a dedicated and hard-working group of people. Thank you everyone in Nanaimo who has ever done a shift swap with me so that I could meet my deadline or avoid the dreaded early morning Sunday ferry.

Special thanks to Kari Jonker, who came up with the design idea for The Moon card. And to you, Chris Parry, for patiently teaching me card meanings.

Liz, thanks for all the rides and conversations. I will miss those 4 a.m. Tarot readings.

I am very proud to be published by Schiffer Publishing, and thank my editor Dinah Roseberry for all her guidance and Pete Schiffer for allowing me the chance to prove myself.

Pamela "Pixie" Coleman Smith deserves all my gratitude as she has left behind a legacy. Her artwork has made the *Rider-Waite Tarot* deck one of the most widely known decks of recent decades. I follow humbly in her footsteps.

Lastly, I would like to thank you, everyone who has ever picked up a Tarot deck and really looked at the artwork.

Let the journey begin.

Contents

Acknowledgments	4
Contents	5
Preface	7
Introduction	8
Tarot Spreads	10

The Major Arcana 13

0 The Fool	14
1 The Magician	16
2 The High Priestess	18
3 The Empress	20
4 The Emperor	22
5 The Hierophant	24
6 The Lovers	26
7 The Chariot	28
8 Strength	30
9 The Hermit	32
10 The Wheel of Fortune	34
11 Justice	36
12 The Hanged Man	38
13 Death	40
14 Temperance	42
15 The Devil	44
16 The Tower	46
17 The Star	48
18 The Moon	50
19 The Sun	52
20 Judgment	54
21 The World	56

The Minor Arcana 58

Ace of Wands	59
Two of Wands	61
Three of Wands	62
Four of Wands	64
Five of Wands	66
Six of Wands	68
Seven of Wands	70
Eight of Wands	72
Nine of Wands	74
Ten of Wands	75
Page of Wands	77
Knight of Wands	78
Queen of Wands	79
King of Wands	81
Ace of Cups	83
Two of Cups	85
Three of Cups	87
Four of Cups	88
Five of Cups	90
Six of Cups	91
Seven of Cups	92
Eight of Cups	94
Nine of Cups	96
Ten of Cups	98
Page of Cups	100
Knight of Cups	101
Queen of Cups	103
King of Cups	105

Ace of Swords	107
Two of Swords	109
Three of Swords	111
Four of Swords	113
Five of Swords	114
Six of Swords	116
Seven of Swords	118
Eight of Swords	120
Nine of Swords	121
Ten of Swords	122
Page of Swords	124
Knight of Swords	126
Queen of Swords	128
King of Swords	130
Ace of Pentacles	132
Two of Pentacles	134
Three of Pentacles	136
Four of Pentacles	137
Five of Pentacles	139
Six of Pentacles	141
Seven of Pentacles	143
Eight of Pentacles	145
Nine of Pentacles	147
Ten of Pentacles	149
Page of Pentacles	151
Knight of Pentacles	153
Queen of Pentacles	154
King of Pentacles	156

Conclusion 158
Bibliography 159

Preface

It was the concept of hats that brought *The Cook's Tarot* into being. I was taking my dog for a walk on a particularly cold and windy day, when one thing led to another. "I wish I had a hat," slowly and curiously turned into, "I have way too many hats," metaphorically speaking, of course.

"He wears many hats" is a phrase that refers to a person who does many different kinds of jobs. That is how I felt. Each thing that I did, or was interested in pursuing, seemed to require the wearing of a different hat. There was no common thread to provide the link between all my responsibilities, passions, and interests. I worked as a nurse in an emergency department, I loved to cook, I had studied art and still continued to paint, and I was re-visiting the Tarot, which I had put aside because of its seemingly scary accuracy when I was a young adult, and looking for anything that would help with love-torn dilemmas.

I decided, there and then, that I needed one big hat—a floppy and all encompassing piece of symbolic headgear. *The Cook's Tarot* was born. It seemed a perfect way to paint, study the cards, and develop a theme about cooking and food.

That was seven years ago, and the gods tend to laugh at our plans. I had no idea that when you create a Tarot deck, you actually live through and learn every one of the cards as they become individual life lessons. This deck has evolved. It is not a culinary guide, or about recipes and wine pairing. It does, however, celebrate the cooks: those who gather, create, and serve food as physical and spiritual nourishment for others.

I believe that the kitchen is the heart of the home. The kitchen table is the meeting place where we are invited to gather together. In this age of religious questioning, it has become the spiritual version of church, where we laugh and cry together as we solve the problems of the world around us. It is a safe place to begin this journey towards enlightenment—that moment when you "get it" and you know your place at the table.

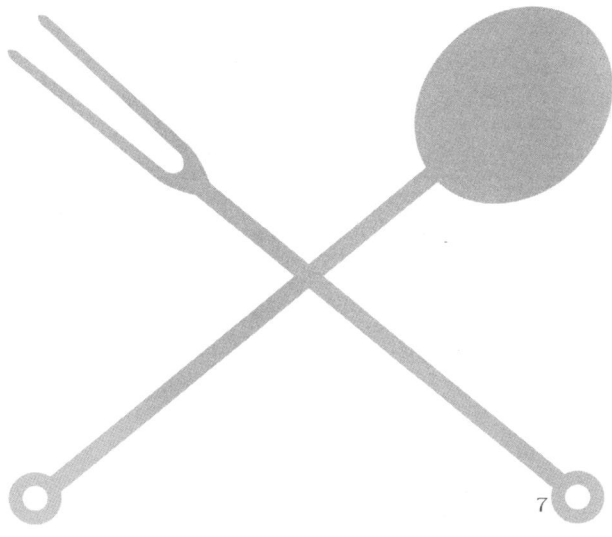

Introduction

The origin of Tarot is uncertain. Some say it dates back to the times of The Knights Templar and earlier. European Tarot was earliest recorded in 1505 as Tarocchi in Italy and Taraux in France. These games were mostly for the entertainment of court nobility and were derived from an earlier form of the game called Trionfi, or Triumphs. In 1920, the *Order of The Golden Dawn* was created and took the lead in organizing Tarot as we know it today. The Rider-Waite Tarot deck has become a modern day icon, and a standard for Tarot symbolism and interpretation. This classic work was illustrated by Pamela "Pixie" Coleman Smith, and it is her legacy that lives on, and whose standards I have followed in the creation of *The Cook's Tarot*.

A standard Tarot deck has 78 cards. It is divided into two parts. The Major Arcana, or "big secrets," comprise the first 22 cards and The Minor Arcana, or "little secrets," are contained in the other 56 cards.

The Major Arcana, numbered from 0 The Fool, to 21 The World, contain the major milestones, or archetypes that we must encounter in the journey towards achieving an understanding of our connection to the physical, emotional, and spiritual world that we inhabit. This is called "obtaining awareness." It is for some a constant condition, and for others, only fleeting glimpses are ever achieved.

The Minor Arcana, or little secrets, are divided much like a typical deck of playing cards. There are four suits: Wands, Cups, Swords, and Pentacles. They can correspond with the clubs, hearts, spades, and diamonds that most people are familiar with. Each suit has four court cards, a King and Queen, and a Knight and Page, which when combined, represent the familiar Jack. The Fool represents the Joker, or the Wild Card. There are then forty "pips," or regular cards, numbered from one, or ace, to ten. There are those who can perform Tarot readings with ordinary playing cards as they relate the qualities of one deck to the other.

The Minor Arcana represent the situations of daily life that we come in contact with. They challenge different aspects of existence, but must be understood in order to gain insight into personal motives and behavioral options, depending on how the cards are chosen and arranged. These situations are not set in stone. Each person will react differently and obtain what advice their particular situation requires.

The Wands hold fire energy and address creative matters, often related to career choices and artistic inspiration. The Cups are vessels, therefore related to the element of water, and speak to all those shifting, changing emotional issues. Swords are sharp, and often double-edged; they slice through the air; they are about communication, logical thinking, and control. The Pentacles are based on the element earth. They represent the senses, as well as financial or worldly concerns.

The Cook's Tarot is created along the same design, with the Major and Minor deck structure and associated court and pip cards. Traditionally, the pip cards were displayed as decorative elements. Pamela Coleman Smith, however, illustrated each card with a specific scene complete with its associated symbolism. I have studied dozens of decks formatted in this tradition, and find that all too many of them take a very literal approach to the interpretation, and end up being simply clones of the original.

I began my journey of Tarot deck creation thinking that I wanted to make a set of cards that I could personally relate to. My background is in healthcare, and I have worked in both pediatric and adult intensive care units and emergency wards. I had no use for anything other than hard facts and reality. No fairies, dragons, or cute kittens for me, please. I chose a theme that appealed to me. Cooking. My thought was that once I understood the inherent meaning of the card, I could transpose the images into a culinary theme. The resultant images would act as a psychic Rorschach, or ink blot test, in which the viewer would bring their own life experiences into the interpretation. The challenge appealed to me in an artistic and academic way.

I set to work and, after six years, completed 78 hand-painted images made from gouache (an opaque water-based paint) on watercolor canvas pads. My approach was completely systematic. I started in sequence, and the first image was The Fool. After the Major Arcana, I started on the court cards, again in sequence of their suits. The Minor Arcana was treated the same way. Finished all the Aces and then all the twos, threes, and so on. My last card was the Ten of Pentacles, and it took about a month to even begin to know how to relate to it.

During those six years strange things started to happen. I found that I was living the experiences of the cards. After two unsatisfactory paintings, the Three of Swords practically painted itself when I found out that a friend had died on Valentine's Day. The Seven of Cups leaped onto the page during a bitter falling out. The Nine of Wands, same thing, except with a business relationship, instead of family. The dogs in our lives also found their way in, especially in the Moon card. The deck was no longer just based on a culinary theme, but instead the theme was based on me. The cards took over my life and I had to closely examine how I felt. I deeply believe that the cooks of the world offer more than just physical nourishment. If you cook with awareness, you are also nurturing the spirit. It is a gift for humanity and a way of expressing a love of life, art, and beauty. It is a celebration of the senses.

Now, here is where it started to get tricky. I decided that when it came time to actually write about the cards, (by this time Schiffer Publishing had offered me a contract) that I would take a different approach. I used the *Anna K Tarot* deck, which I greatly admire, and after shuffling, picked a card to write about. I was shocked at what had found its way into each card when I started, again, to research the symbolism of the "Key Elements." Where I had intended purely compositional elements, I found profound insights and new understandings. I cannot explain it. Even now, I have to physically shut my eyes to even say out loud, "Something guided me," because, well, that goes against the grain of hard-boiled reality.

In conclusion, I have to say that despite all the theories about the collective unconscious, spiritual wisdom of the ages and ink blots, I really don't know how the Tarot works. I just know that it does. If you open your mind and ask for guidance, when you shuffle these cards, and lay them out, you will get it. Go ahead and give it a try.

Tarot Spreads

Tarot can be thought of as a universal language, because of the use of archetypal images, numbers, and symbols that come into play when doing a reading. Like any language, it takes time to first learn the basic meanings, and then the more subtle ones. There is no "proper" way to gain understanding, it just comes from repeated study and examination. The more comfortable you become with each formal card meaning, the more you can let go of it and then trust your intuition. There are endless amounts of "Spreads" available. A Spread is a system or way of laying out the cards that speaks to what the "querent," or person asking the question, wants to find out. There are many books available on creating or using different spreads. I suggest that you read as many of them as you can.

The first step is, of course, to obtain a deck of cards. It is a myth that your first deck has to be given to you. You need to find one in which the images resonate, and you find it easy to understand the symbolism.

Treat the cards with proper respect. Store them carefully, and use some sort of ritual when approaching them for guidance. Many people use a special cloth to lay their cards on during a reading. You can also use this material to wrap the cards in for storage and protection. You need a quiet space, and enough time that you can clear your mind of distractions. Sit with both feet on the ground. Some people light a candle, or spray a bit of lavender for clarity before they begin.

Shuffle the cards in a way that is comfortable. I hold the deck in my right hand and let them fall in different sequences into my left hand. When you are through, lay the cards in a single pile. If any cards fall out, put them aside, because they have a meaning that will be revealed during the reading. Using your non-dominant hand, separate the deck into three piles. Then using the same hand, pick them back up and put them together in a way that feels "right." The deck is then read either by you, or a reader, by picking the cards from the top of the deck and laying them out into a specific pattern, or spread. Another way is to just spread the cards out in a fan like shape and pick the cards that way. There are no hard and fast rules.

When approaching a reading, the more specific your question, the more direct an answer you will receive. It is not fortune telling, so questions related to how to approach an issue are more useful than vague, "Will I be happy, will I be rich?" scenarios.

The cards in this deck are paintings and considered works of art. I do not supply any "reverse" meanings for cards that are upside down. Personally, I turn all the cards upright. When a card is played upside down, the meaning is taken to be the opposite of the intended one. I prefer to think of all situations as having an inherent duality. Nothing is ever completely black and white, or, good and bad. I, therefore, describe the "shadow" side to a card, such as night is the shadow to day, and back is the shadow to front. It takes both sides of a situation to describe it entirely. It depends on your personal circumstances as to what aspect holds the most significance to you. If you choose to read with reversals, that is perfectly all right and will not detract from the essence of the reading.

CARD OF THE DAY

The simplest reading is to use a single card, commonly called the "card of the day." This is a good way to learn the deck as you focus on one card and what it means to you. Study the image, noticing the direction that the figures face, the colors, their facial expressions, and their body language. After reading the formal definition, then examine what that card means to you. Does it seem positive or negative? What sort of story can you tell about it? Does it remind you of anything? Keep the image in your head as you go through the day, and you will find circumstances that relate to that card. For instance, if you picked The Page of Pentacles, you are being asked to be patient and to study the situation carefully and gather all the metaphorical ingredients or facts before making a decision.

THE THREE-CARD SPREAD

A three-card spread is also good for simple "What do I need to know?" questions. Lay the cards out in the following way:

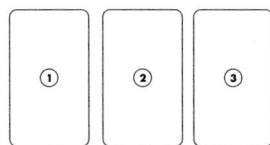

1. The current situation.
2. Factors in the past that have influenced the situation.
3. Future outcome.

THE FIVE-CARD SPREAD

A five-card spread is good for gaining deeper insight into a situation. Lay the cards out as follows:

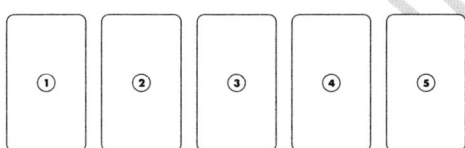

1. The present—what you know about the situation.
2. Hidden factors—the unknown.
3. Strengths that you can utilize.
4. Outcome.
5. Consequences, or, how it will affect you.

The Ten-Card Spread

The traditional Celtic Cross or Ten-Card Spread is used for divination or trying to understand what options are available in order to proceed in the right direction.

1. The heart of the matter, or the issue at hand.
2. What crosses it, or those things that either work for or against the issue.
3. Crown. Conscious feelings.
4. Beneath. The unconscious factors at work.
5. Past influences.
6. Future influences that are either just beginning or will soon affect the situation.
7. Self. How you feel about things.
8. House. How others see you. What friends and family think or feel.
9. Hopes and Fears.
10. Outcome.

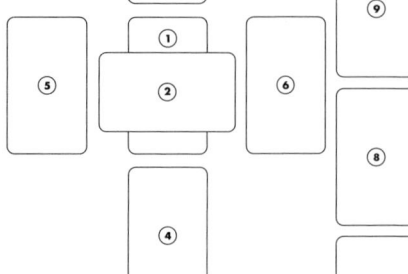

Other cards can be drawn if further clarification is needed with the outcome.

The Cook's Tarot Maitre D' Spread

Maitre d' is short for "Maitre d'Hotel," which means "Master of the Hotel." It is based on a human form with the main "body" consisting of the head, heart, and guts of the situation. The legs represent directions, the arms represent momentum, and, of course, the hat represents wisdom.

Lay the cards out in the following order.

1. The heart of the matter, or the present situation.
2. Head. What you would like as an outcome.
3. Foundation. Core issues.
4. Past directions, or influences.
5. Future direction, or influences.
6. Blockages, weaknesses.
7. Opportunities, strengths.
8. Wisdom. What you need to know.

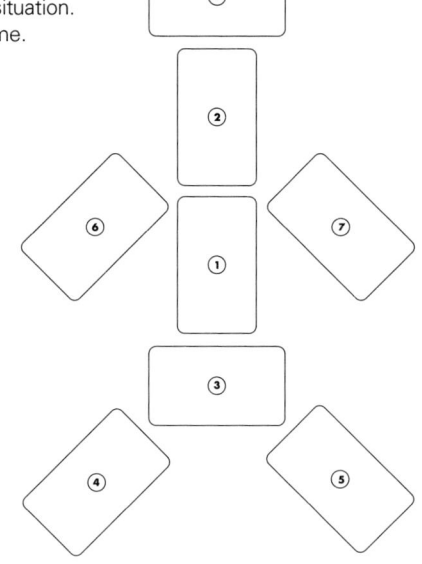

The Major Arcana

The Major Arcana are the first 22 cards of a Tarot deck. They have been called "The Fool's Journey" or "The Royal Road," as they depict a journey from a state of unenlightenment or ignorance towards a state of awareness or knowledge.

The Fool is numbered zero (0), and represents "Everyman," or the one who is on the journey. The remaining 21 cards represent archetypes, which is another name for a universally understood symbol, term, statement, or pattern of behavior. For instance, The Emperor is the archetype for masculine power and control, and The Devil is the archetype for the baser side of human nature.

The cards, numbered 1 to 21, represent the characters, situations, and life forces that make up the significant milestones that we must pass in order to fulfill a life's mission. They represent challenges that are both physical and philosophical, and address intellectual, emotional, and spiritual issues. They are seen as the trump cards in a reading, as they are generally unavoidable, and cannot be diverted from. They are the immovable forces that we must come to terms with.

In *The Cook's Tarot*, the traditional meaning of each card has been strictly adhered to, but the visual interpretation has been altered to suit more modern times and the vision of this deck. The Fool in standard *R.W.S.* tradition is male—here she is female, as are The Hierophant and The Hermit. Temperance is male, and there is no white horse and skeleton in the Death card. The Star is in a bathtub, and the Tower is a pile of dishes and a fallen cake.

There was no conscious intention for designing them this way, no political statement. This is just the way they presented themselves to me. Who can argue?

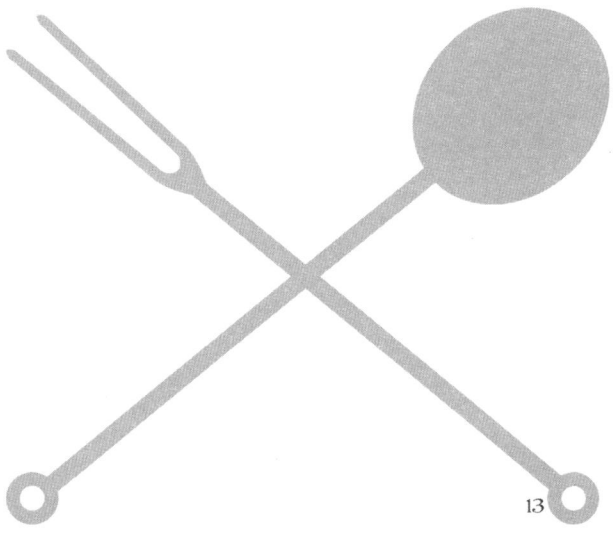

0 THE FOOL

Arcanum: 0
Zodiac Affinity: Uranus

Dancing with joyous abandon, a young woman twirls around in her kitchen. She is wearing dancing slippers and a skirt that balloons out in a series of widening circles. She grabs a wooden spoon in one hand, and a bag of sugar in the other, as she impulsively decides to do some baking. As she hoists the bag into the air, its contents spill out. Most of the sugar magically finds its way to nearby baskets and jars, while the rest of it lands on the floor. A little dog is standing close to her as if getting ready to taste the unexpected treat. Our young Fool (for this is who she is) is unaware of the chaos. She remains happily oblivious to the possibility of failure. She has all the confidence of youth, and has not yet learned about the consequences of rash behavior.

KEY ELEMENTS

Dancing Clothes: The flamboyant skirt is made to look like a series of circles, representing the number zero, physically seen as "0." In numerological terms, zero is seen as the beginning of a cycle that leads to great transformation. The circle is symbolic of the void that contains both nothingness and boundless potential. The circle of life has no beginning or end, but individually, we embark on many journeys in a lifetime. The widening bands of the skirt are synonymous with the widening of our consciousness as we complete each cycle and begin another.

The Ballet Slippers: Just for fun.

Spilled Sugar: The alchemical use for raw or unrefined sugar has been to "dispel evil influences." It is considered to have water, therefore, feminine energy. The use of sugar in this card is to associate the character of The Fool with the sweetness of a substance that is very delicious, but should be used with caution. It is naive to expect that one can eat a lot of sugar without certain consequences.

The act of spilling anything suggests certain carelessness, and in this card, it is due to over exuberance rather than laziness.

Dog: A longtime symbol of faithfulness and protection. In this card, it is a tribute to my sister's beagle, a truly neurotic soul, who lived through many cycles of change, both literally and figuratively. The little dog is The Fool's companion, sometimes a voice of reason and other times, just along for the ride.

CARD MEANING

If you knew in advance about all the work, effort, and problems that lay ahead, you would never start a new project. Sometimes, "ignorance is bliss," and it takes energy and enthusiasm to galvanize yourself into a new beginning.

A Tarot deck follows The Fool's (or Everyman's) journey from just such a state of youthful unawareness to a destination of maturity. It describes a cycle of completion with all the lessons learned along the way. The Fool is, therefore, zero (0), full of potential, waiting to be filled. Uranus is the planet in the Zodiac that is associated with The Fool; it is no accident that it represents freedom, independence, and a disregard for rules.

When you draw this card in a reading, it signifies the start of a hugely transformational cycle. Due to its extreme nature, it should come with a warning label, because the shadow side of this card is carelessness, The Fool's downfall. When you are visited by The Fool, you are being invited on a journey. It could involve the start of a new career, a new relationship, a new philosophical approach, or a literal trip of significant distance. Go! Take that leap of faith, dance around your kitchen, bake a cake and start packing. It is time to find delight in your very existence.

It is important to know the difference between anticipating events and over-thinking. Take a lesson from the sugar, and try not to spill things.

KITCHEN WISDOM

There is joy in cooking when you do not fear the failure.

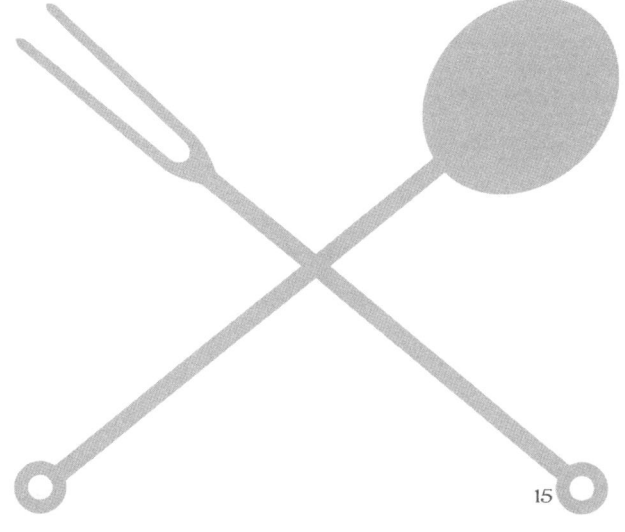

1 The Magician

Arcanum: 1
Zodiac Affinity: Mercury

THE MAGICIAN

A young Magician dressed as a chef gazes upwards towards the blooming lemniscate that he holds in his outstretched right hand. His left hand points downwards towards the assorted tools of his trade. He wears a white shirt that is partially covered by a red apron. Behind him, there is a stylized window with metal bars that have turned into further blooming tendrils.

Key Elements

Lemniscate: The figure "8" turned on its side represents the symbol for infinity. It is a depiction of cycles that are in continuous motion, having no beginning or end. This Magician holds the lemniscate at the point of intersection between the two loops, implying that he grasps the connection between past, present, and future actions. The leaves indicate that not only is time endless, but so is life.

Kitchen Implements Representing the Four Suits of Tarot:

PITCHER: The suit of Cups and the primordial element of water. This speaks to the heart and taps into our emotions.

KNIFE: The suit of Swords, element of air, addresses the mind and matters of communication.

DISH: The suit of Pentacles, element of earth, speaks to our bodies and the five senses.

ROLLING PIN: The suit of Wands, element of fire, represents the passion in our souls and fosters creative pursuits.

The Magician pulls the powers of the universe towards him, and, as they pass through his body, they become directed to the physical plane. Mind, heart, body, and soul are derived from air, water, earth, and fire, leading to the phrase, "as above, so below."

Colors:

WHITE: The shirt of this Magician is white, representing the innocence of The Fool on his journey

RED: The apron is red, implying a more worldly experience and knowledge.

Card Meaning

The Magician is associated with Mercury, messenger of the Roman gods. It is understood that The Magician is privy to the secrets of the gods, and he in turn translates them to us lowly mortals. In a reading, this card represents the bridge between the world of the spirit and the world of humanity. In practical terms, The Magician is the archetypal achiever. He is able to trust his instincts and facilitate new beginnings.

This card represents the beginning of significant events. Our actions will affect things that could impact the rest of our lives. It is necessary to consider the meaning of the lemniscates and understand the nature of Karma. Past actions affect our present responses, which in turn affect our future destiny, ad-infinitum.

So, this is not a card to be taken lightly. Knowledge is power in this situation. This is not just simply knowing the facts, although that is very important, but also self-knowledge, the ability to listen to your inner voice, or instinct. You are encouraged to realize your full potential and understand that possibility is unlimited if you start on your journey with an open heart.

The shadow side to this card is that knowledge and power can be abused. The great achiever could become the great manipulator. No one can truly have all the answers to everything. The key to success is not to deceive yourself, or others, about your ability.

Kitchen Wisdom

True alchemy involves a sense of rightness and timing.
Trust your instincts; test the temperature of the air as well as the oven.

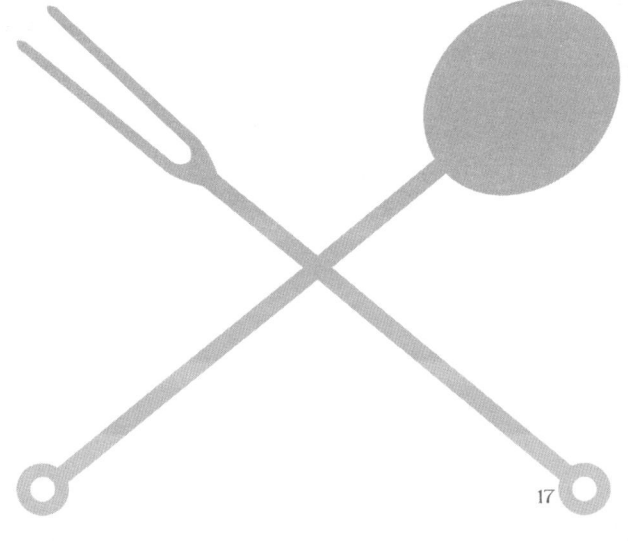

2 The High Priestess

Arcanum: 2
Zodiac Affinity: Moon

Night is falling, and a crescent moon is moving upwards in the sky. Through the filmy curtain of a restaurant window we see a woman partially revealed. The lines of her clothing seem to melt and blend with the folds of the loose drapery. The "Open" sign is lit, and she is busy lighting candles, preparing for the first customers of the evening. A small orange cat is watching these activities, as he is never very far from his mistress. This is a very understated image for one of the most important figures of the Major Arcana, but, The High Priestess (for this is who she is) likes to keep a low profile, revealing her secrets only when she is ready to do so.

Key Elements

Curtain: Used to represent the veil, as in the "secrets behind the veil." A veil is usually seen as a barrier for a person, place, or thing. The idea is that to part the veil, will reveal the secrets. A bridal veil is traditionally a symbol of virginity, and for the bridegroom to raise the veil implies a conjugal union. The phrase, "to draw a veil over" means to conceal or keep certain facts from public knowledge. To "go beyond the veil" means to enter the holiest of holy places in the tabernacle or temple. To "cross over the veil" means to enter that unknowable state that follows death. The veil is then the barrier between the "land of the living and the land of the dead." In Tarot archetypes The High Priestess is the keeper of the secrets that lie behind the veil. Meaning that she alone knows how to access the wisdom of the ages, that universal stream of unconscious knowledge otherwise known as intuition.

Candles: The symbolic meaning of a candle is dependent on the context in which it is shown. A religious votive candle acts as a symbol of spiritual devotion, and a wedding candle speaks to the bond between a couple. In general though, a candle is a symbol for triumph over darkness. It literally lights the way and can be seen to represent the intellect, enlightenment and awareness. The High Priestess is lighting the candles in order to guide us in our search for the truth. This soft lighting also corresponds with her affinity with the moon, and sets the stage for intimate revelations.

Card Meaning

The High Priestess is known as "the Queen of borrowed light" because of her close affinity to the moon, which reflects the light of the sun. The sun symbolizes illumination, or the act of being filled with knowledge and awareness. The moon plays the opposite role and tends to hide its secrets in the dark shadows, waiting for time to pass in order for them to be revealed by the breaking dawn. It is passive energy compared to the vitality of the sun.

The moon is strongly associated with the feminine, and, as it has a powerful influence over tidal systems, it also governs all emotional energy that is tied to the water element. The High Priestess is the female archetype in that she is the emblem of receptive powers.

She has been described as the female counterpart to The Magician. He looks to the heavens for information that he passes on as a messenger. She looks to the heavens and seems to intuitively acquire the wisdom of the ages. That wisdom is only revealed to those who "go beyond the veil." The High Priestess is also associated with The Hierophant, as she is the keeper of knowledge that has been passed on in a timeless fashion.

When you draw this card in a reading, it symbolizes a very important dawning of awareness. A secret of some kind will be revealed and you will be called upon to use all your intuitive powers in order to manage the situation.

The High Priestess is a card that requires patience, as results cannot be forced, but rather must be revealed. It is a card that tells you to trust your instincts and let them guide your decision-making processes. The shadow side to this card occurs when secrets are used to hurt others, and they take on a malicious quality.

The "Open" sign on the card implies that not only is the establishment open for business, but we must likewise open our minds in order to look beyond our own veils, disguised as rational thinking.

Kitchen Wisdom

When you are steaming mussels or clams,
never eat one that you have to actively pry open.
If they do not open when they are ready,
they will not be good for you.

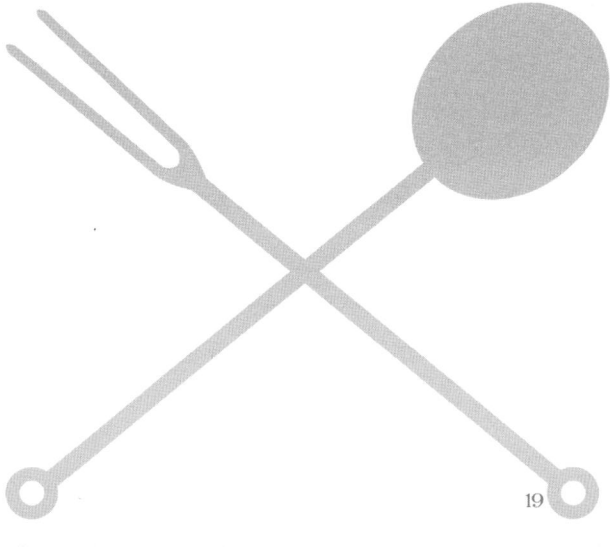

3 THE EMPRESS

Arcanum: 3
Zodiac Affinity: Venus

A pregnant woman is on her deck, enjoying the sunshine. She is resting on a luxurious red pillow, and holds a full glass of water in one hand and an apple in the other. At her feet are baskets of freshly picked produce, corn, apples, and pomegranates. In the distance, there is a view of fields that are the same golden color as her hair. Half of the wooden deck is bathed in sunshine; the other half is covered in shadow. It is a captured moment of time, all movement has stopped, even the wind is motionless. She will soon open her eyes and activity will begin again.

KEY ELEMENTS

Pregnancy: The Empress is the mother archetype. She represents fertility and abundance. The gravid womb symbolizes not only actual childbirth, but also the growth and development of new ideas and projects. It implies boundless potential.

Water: Symbolic of life-giving forces. It has been said that dreaming of a glass of water symbolizes protection from harmful forces. Water is fundamental in creating and sustaining life, but it is equally destructive as it drowns and destroys life as well.

Baskets of Produce: Full baskets mean that the harvest has been successful and no one will go hungry. In metaphorical terms, it describes an unconditional love and generosity of spirit. Mother Earth has provided for all.

Red Cushion: A symbol of luxury and passion. The Roman goddess Venus (known as Aphrodite in Greece) is associated with The Empress, and is known in popular culture as the "goddess of beauty and love." She is associated with female sensuality, an appreciation of "the finer things" found in culture and art.

Eyes Closed: This is a literal interpretation, and hint of playfulness on the part of the artist, as it describes the phrase, "a pregnant pause." It speaks to that moment just before a significant thought or subject is broached. The potential for creativity is implied in the silence. The eyes will open, the respite will be over, and all things will come to their fruition.

Card Meaning

The Empress card is the universally understood symbol of motherhood. It implies not only the literal possibility of pregnancy and childbirth, but also the metaphorical birthing of creative endeavors. The Empress is associated with the natural world as she is Mother Earth. She is responsible for not only the fields and streams, but also the harvest and all the abundant goodness that life has to offer.

This is generally a very positive card to get in a reading because it asks you to connect with nature and your feminine side. It encourages a nurturing approach to a situation whether it involves family matters or projects that you are involved in. Patience and love are the keys to success.

The shadow side to this card is inherent in all mothers. What starts out as a protective influence can become overbearing and possessive. If there are negative associations with this card, you need to take a step backwards and close your eyes. Allow life to find its own way without your constant guidance. It will happen, as life will always triumph. Open your eyes and the moment will resume.

Kitchen Wisdom

"If Mamma ain't happy, ain't nobody happy."

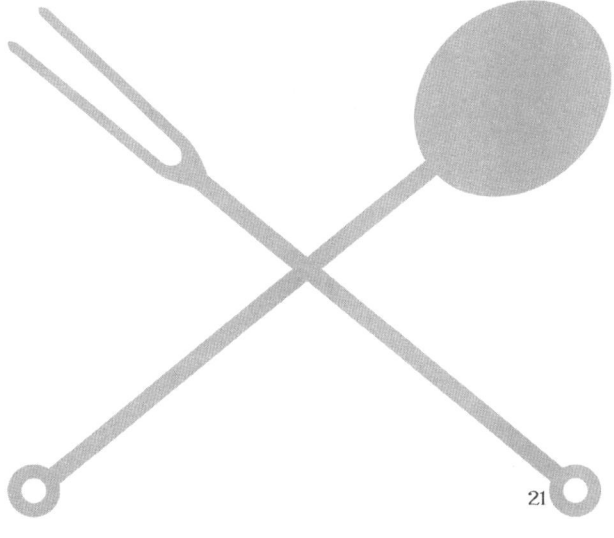

4 The Emperor

Arcanum: 4
Zodiac Affinity: Aries

THE EMPEROR

A modern-day Emperor is seen ruling over the barbecue. He clutches the grilling utensils with both hands as if ready for battle. The skewers of food are aligned with military precision as they stand at attention over the searing coals. Standing guard beside The Emperor is a stone figure of Aries, the Ram. In the background, fantastical sand castles rise up on an empty beach. His regal stature, and the wearing of a beach towel as a cloak, shows that he is taking even this simple task very seriously. This sovereign is always on duty.

Key Elements

The Ram: The Emperor is associated with the first sign of the Zodiac, Aries the Ram. It is a fire sign that calls for forceful action. Aries rules the head and is therefore strong-willed and authoritarian. Mars, associated with the god of war, is the planet that rules Aries. It is no accident that the head and horns of the ram are depicted as the astrological symbol. The persona of the ram is head down, charging forward and ready to butt any obstacles out of the way. In this card, the ram symbolizes force and inflexibility.

Sand Castles: A castle is a walled and defended city. In folklore it often holds a treasure or a prisoner that needs to be rescued. A sand castle is much less significant as it is the stuff of imagination and creativity. Sand itself, represents the rational brain, just as water represents its more emotional aspects. A beach, in metaphorical terms, is described as the transition between the physical and the spiritual, as we have to cross the beach to approach the water. For the purposes of this card, sand castles represent the psyche. How you view the structures is significant as to how you view the Emperor. Do the castles seem real? Are they examples of discipline and creativity? Do they show organizational skill? Are they tender examples of family entertainment, or merely the result of a juvenile pastime?

Card Meaning

The Emperor is the archetypal, or universally understood, symbol of authority and leadership. He represents the father figure and is the masculine counterpart to The Empress, who is the archetypal mother figure. Like all fathers, The Emperor has many sides to him. Aries, the first sign in the Zodiac, supplies The Emperor with characteristics of the *firstborn,* such as being independent, strong willed, and self-directed. The concept of *firstborn* also conjures up examples of infant-like behavior, such as energy and enthusiasm on one hand, and impatience, self-absorption, and a demanding nature on the other.

The Emperor card is generally about, "Who is the boss?" You might be working for The Emperor and have to deal with issues of control and demanding expectations. You could be in need of direction and looking for a father figure to guide you, or you might be the boss and have to rule your empire with organizational strength and energy.

When you draw this card in a reading, there is usually a fiery situation that needs to be directed, and it is the Ram, the boss who is going to lead the way. In either case, you are being asked to step up to the plate and control either the situation or your reaction to it.

The shadow side to this card lies in being too dogmatic and inflexible. In order to succeed, you will need to be sensitive to the temperature of the fire. If you are in doubt as to how to do that, find The Empress.

Kitchen Wisdom

A quote from the Roman philosopher, Seneca:
"He is most powerful who has power over himself."

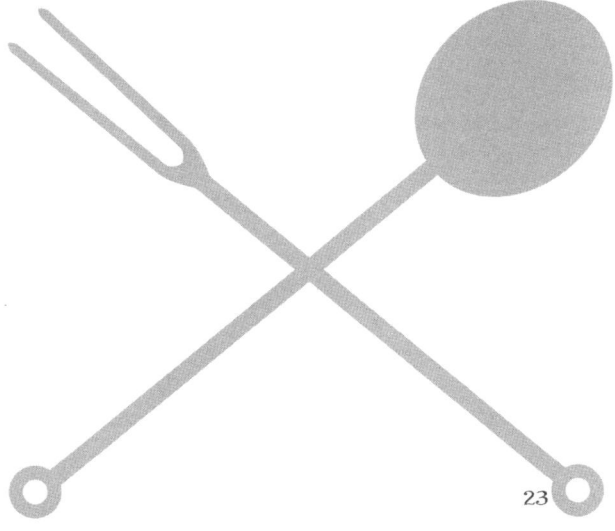

5 THE HIEROPHANT

Arcanum: 5
Zodiac Affinity: Taurus

A woman with a long red scarf around her neck points to a written symbol. She is directing her information towards two seated individuals. The female holds her chin in her hand and looks either tired or bored. The male, who is wearing his hat at the table, is paying close attention. On the table is a single rose in a glass vase. It lies on top of a cloth designed with the pattern of a giant lotus. The keys of wisdom are woven into the pattern of the rug that lies below them. An apple pie lies cooling on the windowsill.

KEY ELEMENTS

Red Scarf: Taurus rules the neck. The scarf symbolizes the connection between the head and the neck, or the connection between the mental and the physical. It combines both the practical aspect of keeping the neck warm and the beauty of a decorative object. Taurus is an earth sign, and therefore fond of creature comforts, but they must also have practical value.

Lotus: Long known as a symbol of enlightenment.

Keys: The keys of knowledge. In traditional papal symbology, *the keys to the Kingdom of Heaven* were shown as two overlapping keys, one of silver and the other of gold. Keys symbolically open the doors to knowledge and wisdom. Not everyone can use these keys. One must study with a Master or spiritual guide until the right to knowledge has been earned.

Apple Pie: A symbol of tradition and family values. It is the ultimate comfort food that offers no surprises. It has become synonymous with conformity, tradition, and secular morality.

CARD MEANING

The Hierophant card talks to the role of student and teacher. It is one of the major milestones in life. On the road to achieving true awareness one must learn the rules from an authority figure. This card is about structure and conformity. It celebrates the status quo. We are not born with all the secrets of wisdom; we have to learn them. This card shows that not everyone is ready to learn, and also that one can learn without the formal trappings of scholarship.

When you draw this card in a reading, it is time to consider your belief system. Are you going in the direction that you believe in or are you blindly following traditional conformity? Are you in need of a mentor in order to achieve your goals?

The shadow side of this card is, of course, blind conformity: following the rules with no thought as to their impact or meaning. This can lead to an abuse of power and a life of bovine self-satisfaction. The perils of an unexamined life!

KITCHEN WISDOM

You have to know the rules before you can break them.

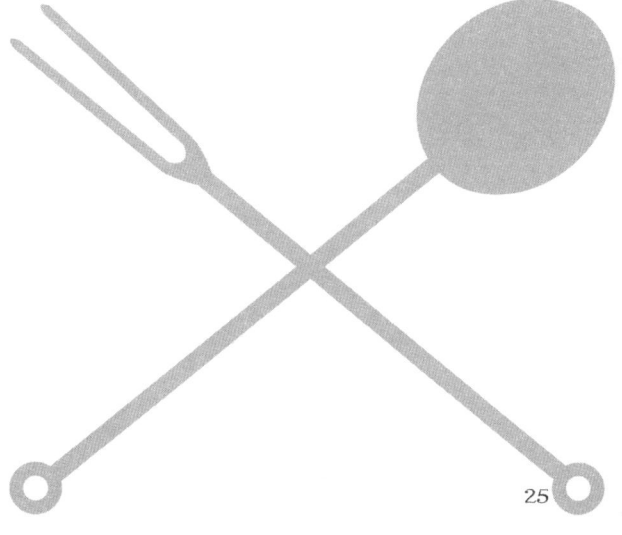

6 THE LOVERS

Arcanum: 6
Zodiac Affinity: Gemini

THE LOVERS

The Lovers are presented with breakfast in bed as they lean back against colorful pillows. The woman's is decorated with an apple motif and the man rests his head on a bed of clouds. An angel stands behind them with widespread arms and bright red wings. The pair seem perfectly at ease, and yet they are not touching, or even looking at each other.

The breakfast tray rests on their laps. There are decisions to be made. Who will have the coffee and who will have the tea? Who will have the cinnamon bun and who will choose the sliced apple? Despite the innocence of the offerings, the woman is eyeing the tray in a speculative manner, as if to say, "Hmmm, I see; but why is there a snake lurking by the teapot?"

KEY ELEMENTS

Snake/Serpent: The snake is a very prominent image in the mythology of various cultures. It represents many good things, such as wisdom, healing, and rejuvenation, and also bad things, such as duplicity, vengefulness, and temptation. The combination of these positive and negative images representing harmony and disharmony, good and evil, fertility and death have allowed the snake to become the perfect image to represent duality. In this card, the serpent coiled around the teapot alludes to the temptation of Adam and Eve in the Garden of Eden. Their innocence was destroyed, but their ability to make choices through the act of free will was gained.

Angel: In traditional cards, the angel Raphael hovers behind a naked couple, arms open as if blessing their union, and represents a connection with the spiritual realm. This is the only card in *The Cook's Tarot* to have an angel in it. It serves the dual purpose of acting as tribute to all previous decks and also represents the supreme act of faith that is entailed in believing that one can find a perfect soul mate and live in blissful harmony. Is it fantasy or reality?

Breakfast Tray: The round tea pot and the cylindrical French press symbolize the yin and yang of a partnership. The healthy apple, also a symbol of temptation, is beside a decadent pastry. The contents of the tray represent the choices that have to be made and this is the inherent message of The Lovers card.

Card Meaning

In Greek mythology, Castor and Pollux were twin brothers. Castor was mortal, and Pollux immortal. When Castor was killed, Pollux went to his father, Zeus, and begged to be allowed to share his immortality with his brother. They then became the constellation known as Gemini. The twins have become the symbol for duality. They represent the light and dark aspects of all things. They are an equal blending of masculine and feminine qualities and define the phrase "separate, yet whole." The Lovers card is associated with the celestial twins in that they imply a need to find your other self in the form of a partner.

On the surface, The Lovers card seems to be about love, partnership, and sexual fulfillment. On a deeper level, this card represents duality and the decisions that need to be made in finding the proper choice of partner, whether on a romantic, business, or platonic level. When you draw this card in a reading, there is a need to make a choice between who or what to love. If you are already involved with a partner, the decisions involve long-term commitment and all the associated issues of home and family. If you are involved with multiple partners, the time has come to make a choice.

This card speaks to all levels of emotional decision making, including business partnerships and choosing a particular pet. The issues of duality are brought into play when you consider the effects of the choice you have made on the rest of your life. The light side of the Lovers will guide you towards a path that compliments your needs without causing disharmony. The dark side of the Twins will have you choosing to live with disharmony for the sake of passion. Use communication, the hallmark of Gemini, as a tool for making the proper decision.

Kitchen Wisdom

"Only in love are unity and duality not in conflict."
~Rabindranath Tagore

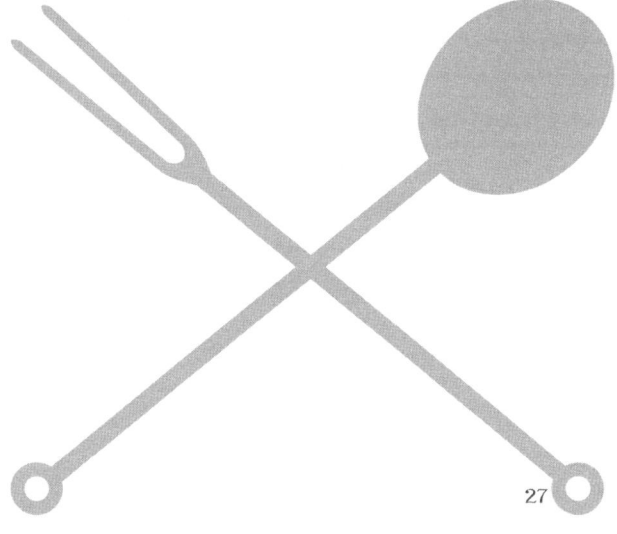

7 The Chariot

Arcanum: 7
Zodiac Affinity: Cancer

THE CHARIOT

A young man dressed in a billowing Magician's coat and blue jeans is pushing a shopping cart with great determination. The scene shifts and changes and the aisles of the supermarket become yellow, tree-painted corridors, the walls dissolve, and a hillside town appears. Undisturbed by these mysterious surroundings, the charioteer adroitly steers his chariot around a blue sphinx that is resting on the floor.

This scene is as multifaceted and complicated, as are the messages found in this seventh card of the Fool's journey. Nothing is as it appears, as anyone attempting to solve the "riddle of the Sphinx" will tell you.

Key Elements

Charioteer: The magically dressed young man is The Charioteer. He embodies the traditional masculine principles of steely determination and goal-oriented single-mindedness. In the world of power and finance, he would be known as a "player." His clothing belies his forceful nature, just as his Zodiac affinity, Cancer; the Crab is a feminine, water sign. He is a mixture of both principles. He has highly charged emotions that he feels he must keep under rigid control in order to achieve his goals. It is the role of the charioteer to steer and guide his way towards finding the right path.

Chariot: A heavy, unwieldy object that has to be pulled and steered in order to get anywhere. Anyone who has maneuvered a loaded shopping cart will see the similarity of this metaphor. In ancient times, a common battle tactic was to attack from the side. A head on collision would amount to no more than a tangle of horses, who would do their instinctive best to avoid just such a situation. This angle of approach provides even more similarities with the Cancer sign, as witnessed by the darting, sideways movements of the crab. The Chariot is a metaphor for traveling. It could be as pragmatic as a journey by car, or have a more esoteric meaning such as a journey through life.

Sphinx: The Sphinx embodies mystery and duality. It is not man, not bird, not beast, and yet all of them at once. There are many tales surrounding the riddle of the Sphinx. Oedipus was said to have solved it. The riddle asked was, "Which creature walks on four legs in the morning, two legs in the afternoon and three legs in the evening?" The answer: "Man—who crawls on all four as a baby, walks on two feet as an adult, and walks with a cane in old age."

CARD MEANING

This is a forceful card that describes forward movement, self-motivation, and also self-control. On one hand, the need for confidence and determination seem to imply a sense of war, struggle, and hard-won victory. On the other hand, there is a sense of knowing when to step aside and take a different approach. Put these two hands together and there is the Sphinx.

When you draw this card in a reading it means that this is a time for decisive action. In order to break out of a non-productive situation, you must choose a path and start on it. Fill your mind with focus and concentration, have a clear goal to journey towards. You will be on the right path, even if at first it does not seem obvious. Accept that whether you crawl, walk upright, or use a cane, you will get there.

The shadow side of this card is found in ego. There is a danger of stretching higher than you are able to reach. One overestimates their ability and becomes reckless. A lack of insight and control can cause the battle to be lost.

KITCHEN WISDOM

Proceed at full speed, but be prepared to step aside.

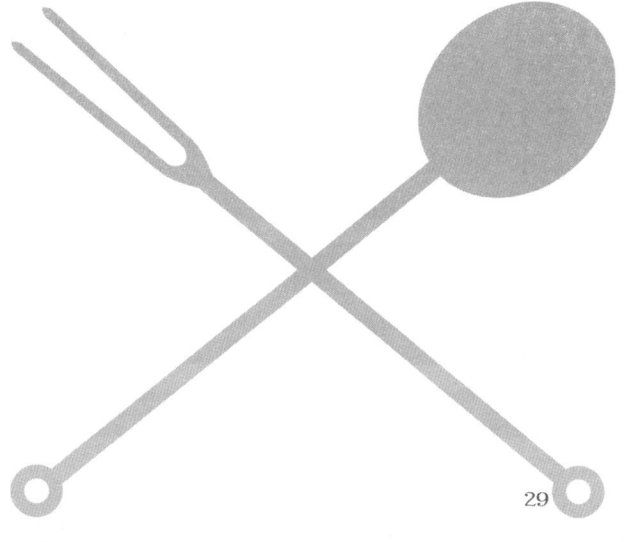

8 Strength

Arcanum: 8
Zodiac Affinity: Leo

There is a steaming bowl of soup on the table. A smiling woman dressed in a pattern of stars and moons is creating a lasso from the spirals of steam. It forms a loosely shaped lemniscate, or infinity symbol, as it wraps around the beast, drawing it closer. The beast already has the body of a man, and is in a position of submission as he holds on to the back of a chair. In the background, a domestic cat is eating from a similar looking bowl.

Key Elements

The Beast: The Strength card is associated with Leo, the lion, king of the jungle, and has become a metaphor describing the id-like part of the mind. The Beast is within us all and addresses our basic primal, or carnal desires. The Beast roars, demanding to be fed. It wants more, more, more. The lion feeding is associated with the human propensity towards excess. The lion tamed is synonymous with discipline and control, the lordly aspects of the king of the jungle.

Lemniscate: The infinity symbol, a figure "8" turned on its side, representing the endless and eternal nature of energy. The steam from the bowl of soup is loosely suggestive of this, as if the mental processes are still being resolved. In Tarot, the sight of the lemniscate tells us that how we respond to the present situation will have significant repercussions in the future. Energy does not change. In this card, the unformed lemniscate indicates more of the internal struggle that is constantly shifting and changing.

Soup: Beethoven wrote in a letter, "only the pure in heart can make good soup" and we all know that "music soothes the savage beast." It is symbolic for succeeding through kindness instead of brutality.

CARD MEANING

The Strength card is the archetype for exerting control over baser human instincts by using mental, rather than physical force. It appeals to our higher senses. The woman is succeeding in taming the beast; meaning that success is possible if one meets the challenges head on, responding with understanding and compassion rather than hostility and aggression.

This card speaks to internal, rather than physical struggles. The issues are very real, however, and they tend to gravitate around the subjects of addiction and excess. They might be related to bodily pleasures, such as food, drugs, and sex, or tend towards the mental excesses of avarice and greed. When you draw this card in a reading, it is a sign that there is a need to address a struggle. Like the smiling sorceress in the card, it will take the magic of personality to gain control of the situation. There is a constant balancing act between self-destruction and self-preservation.

The shadow side of this card is that we can become a bit self-righteous in our purity of thought. We need to be part of humanity, warts and all.

KITCHEN WISDOM

The house cat and the lion are all part of the same family.

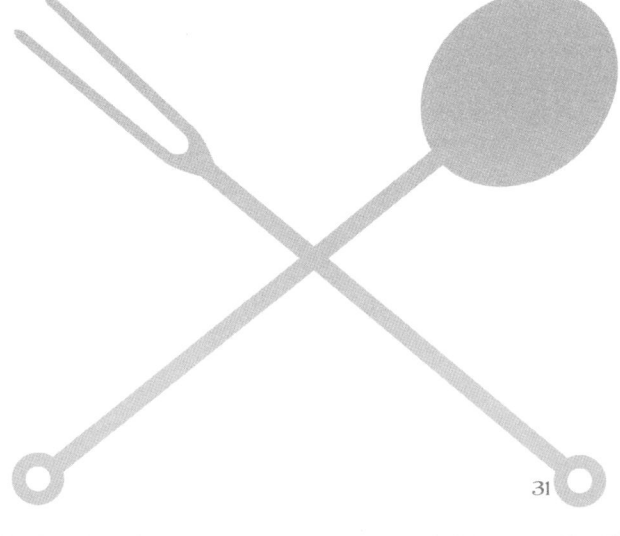

9 THE HERMIT

Arcanum: 9
Zodiac Affinity: Virgo

The stars are shining brightly and the moonlight is reflecting off the water. Magic is in the air. This woman rises from her solitary studies, closes the books, and throws back the curtains that have been obscuring the view. She looks outside, as if seeing the beauty of the night for the first time. It has always been there. She marvels that she has never fully appreciated it before. All this time spent, sequestering herself from the demands of society in order to complete her research, while the night was patiently waiting. She raises a silent toast to the end of one cycle of knowledge and the beginning of another.

KEY ELEMENTS

Books: There are so many books in the world. All that knowledge trapped between all those pages. Today, computers have taken over the role of providing the answers to all questions. There is instant access, available at the touch of a fingertip. The books in this card are symbolic of knowledge that has always been there, but is not available via the "information super-highway." They remind us that research is time-consuming and requires solitary effort. The answers we start out looking for are not always those that are eventually revealed.

Lantern: Literally, a lantern provides light when it is dark. It illuminates the shadowy corners and allows for safe passage. It can also act as a beacon that guides others to us. In this card, the lantern is symbolic of internal reflection. It is shown sitting on a table, lighting the interior of the house, while the moon and stars provide a brilliant display outside.

Curtain: To open the curtains means to open the mind and to look outside one's own narrow perspective. It is time to shake off old customs and values.

CARD MEANING

The Hermit is the ninth card in The Fool's journey towards enlightenment. Nine, in numerological terms, means the end of a cycle, but not yet the beginning of a new one. The Hermit is also associated with Virgo, the virgin. The character of Virgo is analytical as well as skeptical, always gathering information, looking for the perfect solution. The Virgin implies a certain aloof attitude that complements a state of aloneness. This card is about finding the answers by yourself. It implies the end of a cycle of ignorance and confusion.

When you draw this card in a reading, you are being told that this is not the time for careless action, but rather the time to sit quietly and reflect on the situation. It is time to end a previously held belief. This card requires from you the kind of introspection that can only come with peace and solitude. The celebration comes from freeing yourself from preconceived expectations.

The shadow side to The Hermit is found when the isolation becomes harmful, and you cut yourself off from others because you are too caught up with finding Virgo-like perfection. As always, the answer lies in finding a balance. This time the answers are to be found by slowing down and reconnecting with yourself.

KITCHEN WISDOM

Being alone does not have to mean being lonely.

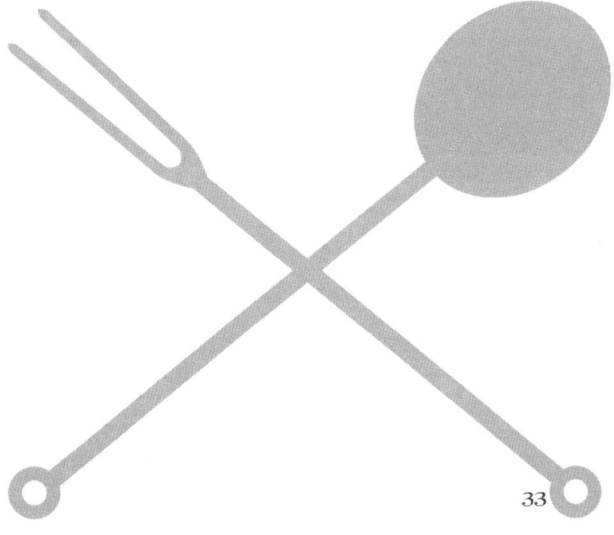

10 The Wheel of Fortune

Arcanum: 10
Zodiac Affinity: Jupiter

THE WHEEL OF FORTUNE

A figure sits alone at a round table that is covered by a cloth depicting a pattern of spokes and a wheel. The chair opposite her is empty, and above her head a utensil rack is madly whirling around. Steam from a teapot and golden stars that seem to spring from nowhere mix together in the air. A star has fallen into the teacup that has been tilted on its side, and another has landed on a loosely knotted purse that sits on the rim of the wheel. There is magic afoot.

Key Elements

Wheels: The circular utensil rack and the patterned table cloth both represent wheels. One is in motion and the other is stable. These are symbolic of the Wheel of Destiny, a popular concept in the Middle Ages and Renaissance. There are two main views as to the nature of this Wheel. The first is that Fortuna, or Fate, turns the wheel, and one has little or no control over one's position on it. Although it may seem completely random and capricious, there is little that can be done about one's fate. The second theory is that as the wheel is always turning, fortunes are always shifting and the outcomes are determined by one's reaction to them. It implies more of a state of free will, as one can actively rise up or fall off the wheel.

Tea Cup: Used for the reading of the tea leaves that settle at the bottom of the cup after the drink has been consumed. Fortunes can be told, depending on the patterns seen in the clumps of tea. A star lies in this cup, predicting a very bright future.

Knotted Purse: Symbolic of fortunes. Although this purse implies coins and wealth, not all fortunes are monetary. Good luck, or good fortune, can involve success in a relationship, career, or even evoke a more positive way of thinking.

CARD MEANING

The Wheel of Fortune card is about sudden changes that seem to appear out of nowhere. The Wheel is governed by Jupiter, the largest planet in the solar system, representing expansive thinking, benevolence, fortune, and good humor. This is important to understand, because not all changes seem to be good. You could be on top of the wheel enjoying life, and suddenly an unexpected event occurs, and there you are, now at the bottom of the wheel. The trick is not to get crushed by it, both literally and figuratively. Whether you call it karma or destiny, there is a continuous movement to events. "What goes around, comes around." How you react to this situation determines the outcome of future events. If you believe the universe is benevolent, your reactions will be naturally more positive.

When you get The Wheel of Fortune in a reading, it is a very auspicious sign. Big things are going to change. If you accept that *fate happens,* you move with the wheel and come out on top. If you struggle against it, you will eventually be rolled over into the mire at the bottom.

A great many people find the safest place to be is at the very hub of the wheel, sitting calmly and watching it go around. This takes a good deal of acceptance of the vicissitudes of life. Others may prefer a wilder ride as they rise and fall.

The shadow side of this card lies in feeling out of control, or even controlled by others. You give up your free will and allow negative things to happen because you think that it is in your destiny and you can do nothing about it.

KITCHEN WISDOM

A good cook understands the law of cycles.
When you have extra food, cook it and put it up in the freezer for those inevitable times when you don't have enough.

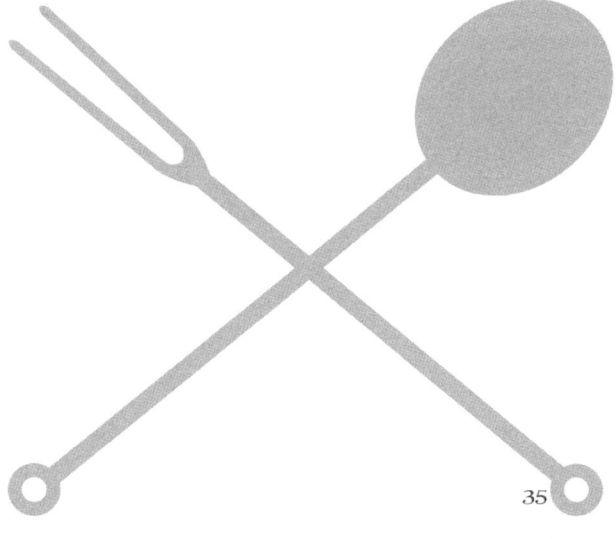

11 JUSTICE

Arcanum: 11
Zodiac Affinity: Libra

A woman is standing barefoot on a bathroom scale that has the traditional Scales of Justice painted on it. She is wearing a filmy sarong that is decorated with a pattern of cherries. In front of her is a bath mat that is patterned with a series of lemons. The light in the card falls so that it bisects both sides of the image, thus forming a stylized hourglass on the scene. This is a non-traditional representation of the Justice card, as Lady Justice is usually seen facing forward, blindfolded, and holding the scales in one hand and a sword in the other. In this instance, the message of objectivity strikes a very personal note as the numbers on the scale are a direct and non-emotional reflection of our physical state. The emotions lie not in the numbers themselves, but in our response to them.

KEY ELEMENTS

Scale: The scales are the only inanimate object pictured in the zodiac. The rest of the symbols are of either people or animals. Legend has it that the ancient Greek goddess of Justice Astraea, or Virgo, went to live among the humans, carrying the Golden Scales of Justice and looking for innocence and purity. Due to human greed and impurity, she left and became the constellation Virgo. The scales beside her formed the constellation Libra. The scales symbolize equality, balance, justice, and harmony. Libra, the zodiac affinity of the Justice card, is an air sign, and therefore uses intellectual means to arrive at solutions. The scales imply a rational and unbiased approach to achieving justice, as there is no room for messy human emotions to distract from the unvarnished truth of the matter.

Feet: Considered sacred in many societies as they are our closest contact to the earth and literally keep us grounded. This card image plays on the phrases, "having both feet on the ground," which means to be well balanced, and, "Stand on you own two feet," which means to be independent and self-sufficient. The feet are bare, which could symbolize a childlike playfulness and innocence, but in reality they are a practical approach to stepping on the scales, as the measurement is more accurate without shoes.

Cherries and Lemons: Life is what you make it: you get the cherries or the lemons. The cherry is sweet, but it has a pit that could cause you to choke and cough. The lemon is sour but can be made into the proverbial lemonade.

Card Meaning

The Justice card is in the exact center of the Major Arcana. The Fool, in his journey, has completed ten steps to get there, and has a further ten steps to go in order to complete his travels. The balance is intentional. He has met the archetypes that speak to issues of personality and emotion and is due to meet those that deal with spirituality and transformation. The Justice card represents a non-judgmental weighing of the facts and information that have been both currently received and those that are waiting to be revealed. Balance is at the fulcrum of how you measure the success or the failure of an endeavor.

When you draw this card in a reading, you are being asked to use objective reasoning when looking at both sides of an issue. There is usually a need to restore balance in your life. The scales can tip in either direction. In this case, the bathroom scales could represent a confirmation of good health, or they could represent being out of alignment due to excessive eating or malnourishment. The Justice card does not tolerate excuses and encourages an unbiased facing of the facts. This card applauds the ability to do whatever is necessary, no matter how difficult, in order to restore physical and emotional well-being.

Kitchen Wisdom

"Face the facts of being what you are,
for that is what changes what you are."
~Soren Kierkegaard

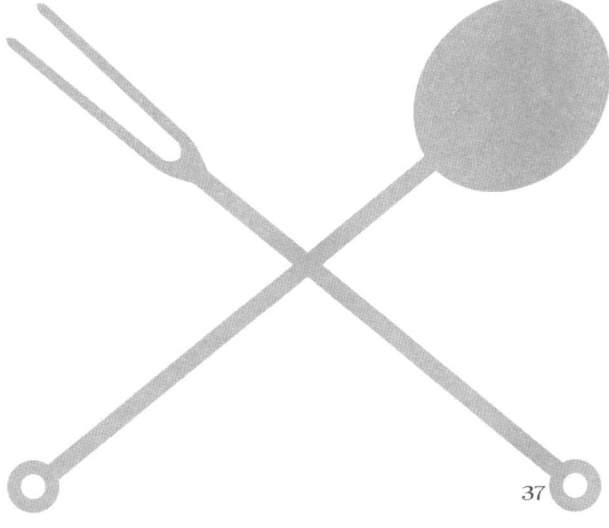

12 THE HANGED MAN

Arcanum: 12
Zodiac Affinity: Neptune

A young man is seen suspended by both legs from the high branches of an apple tree. He appears untroubled and has a serene expression on his face. His right arm is held behind his back and his left arm is extended, palm open, below the fruit. He seems to be waiting for the apples to fall into his hand, even though he could easily reach up and pick them.

KEY ELEMENTS

Apple Tree: This tree is associated with spirituality and knowledge. It is said that the *World Tree*, or the *First Tree*, rooted at the top of the world and nurtured by Gaia, was an apple tree. Odin, in Norse mythology, was thought to have allowed himself to be suspended from just such a tree. He remained there for nine days, wounded and starving, until he noticed the runes that contained all the knowledge in the world below the tree.

Apple: This fruit is rich with symbolism. Because of its spherical shape it has been associated with the concepts of infinity, totality, and unity. Its sweet taste and round shape (associated with female breasts) have caused the apple to be held responsible for the fall of man. The forbidden fruit has become synonymous with sin and temptation. It has also been known as "the fruit of knowledge" and the "apple of discord" to name two other attributes. Apples also contain the notion of duality, as they can be both bitter and sweet at different stages of their formation.

Card Meaning

Neptune is the planet that corresponds most with the ideals of spirituality and self-sacrifice. The god Neptune is ruler of the Seas. These deep waters hold similar dream-like and emotional portents. It is no surprise that they are associated with The Hanged Man, who is the archetype for willing surrender in order to gain knowledge.

The Hanged Man in this card is seen suspended with both legs over the branches of a tree. There is no rope holding him in place, alluding to the fact that he has not been coerced or forced into this position. The gesture is fully intentional and adds a martyred quality to his quest for knowledge. The left hand outstretched symbolizes a search for higher awareness. The passive gesture implies that this is not an active search, but more of a waiting for the knowledge to be revealed. This is a card of paradox, in that the answers that you are looking for can only be revealed when you stop looking. In practical terms it means that you must do the opposite of what seems obvious in order to achieve results.

When you draw this card in a reading it means that it is time to view things from a different perspective. It is a card of non-action, in that it is often wiser to do nothing, than to waste energy on futile activities. You are asked to go passive, to let go of expectations, and to suspend the demands of self-absorption created by the ego.

The shadow side to this card is that martyrdom is not a particularly attractive quality. Suffering can become very self-absorbing and whatever wisdom is gained is also lost. When you get a visit from The Hanged Man, the thing to keep in mind is that he can move at any time. The vision of the world seen from a different angle will never be lost.

Kitchen Wisdom

If you have problems to solve, forget about them and bake a cake instead.

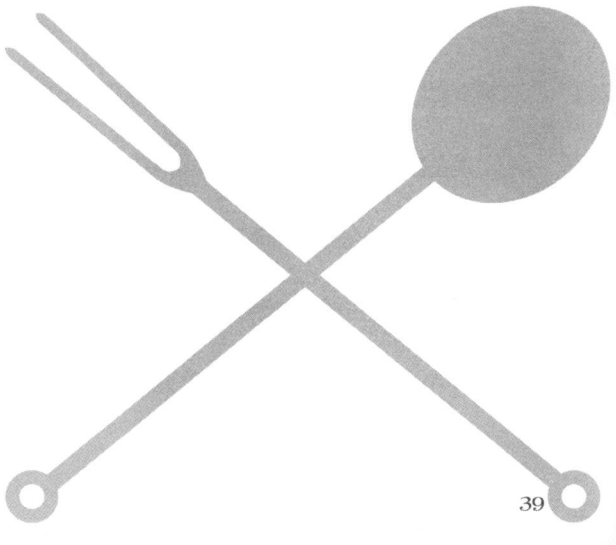

13 Death

Arcanum: 13
Zodiac Affinity: Scorpio

The images on this card address the subject of Death on three levels. There are thirteen little chickens milling around a large pot that has a cleaver resting in it. The implication is that those chickens will eventually end up in the pot, thus perpetuating the food-chain cycle of life and death. A large wishbone crosses the cleaver, casting its shadow on it. This is "the Memento Mori," Latin for, "remember that you will die." It is used by artists as a symbolic reminder of the inevitability of death. Typical images are of a skull or a skeleton. The wishbone adds a lighthearted touch, meaning that it is all not so serious and, out of this ending, wishes may come true. Then there is the feather floating downwards, its shadow also cast upon the waiting pot. The act of death is elevated to an act of transformation, as feathers symbolize higher thought and spiritual progression.

Key Elements

Chickens: A chicken is part of the Chinese zodiac calendar, and to serve a whole bird on Chinese New Year means that the entire family will be brought together in unity. King Henry the IV of France made the declaration that he wanted "no peasant so poor as to not have a chicken in his pot every Sunday." As symbolic elements, they represent the domestic life cycle.

Cleaver: This takes the place of the scythe in traditional Tarot cards: it is the weapon of choice for the Grim Reaper. It represents a cutting or stripping away of all pretension. A reminder that everything must come to a conclusion.

Wishbone: For centuries, pulling on the dried ends of a turkey or chicken *wishbone* until it snapped (the lucky break) would bring good luck to the winner, the one that ended up with the largest piece. Some cultures also use dried wishbones as *dream catchers,* bringing good energy to the sleeper. In this card, the wishbone symbolizes a karmic cycle. The death of a chicken creates a wishbone, which in turn brings good luck and prosperity.

Feather: Ma'at, the Egyptian goddess of justice, would weigh the souls of the newly dead against the weight of a feather to determine the worthiness of their souls. A feather is symbolic of "truth, speed, lightness, flight, and ascension." In this card, it is synonymous with rebirth and continuation.

CARD MEANING

The Death card represents the occurrence of a major change that is brought about by the end of one cycle and the beginning of another. Most often, it is not foretelling a literal death, but rather a significant change, such as the end of one career for a new one, the end of a bad relationship, or even the start of a new way of thinking. It is associated with the zodiac sign Scorpio. The scorpion is known for its *sting of death*, but also for its three forms of mythological transformation—scorpion to serpent to eagle. Scorpio is also a highly sensual sign and signifies sex and intense emotion.

When you draw this card in a reading, you should be very happy. A shift is about to occur, one that is possibly long overdue. It could be very significant and life altering, or more mundane ,like the end of a bad day. The thing to remember is that change is inevitable just like the proverbial "death and taxes." So rather than dread the future, you should embrace what life has to offer.

KITCHEN WISDOM

All endings create new beginnings.
The leftovers from one meal can be the foundation for another.

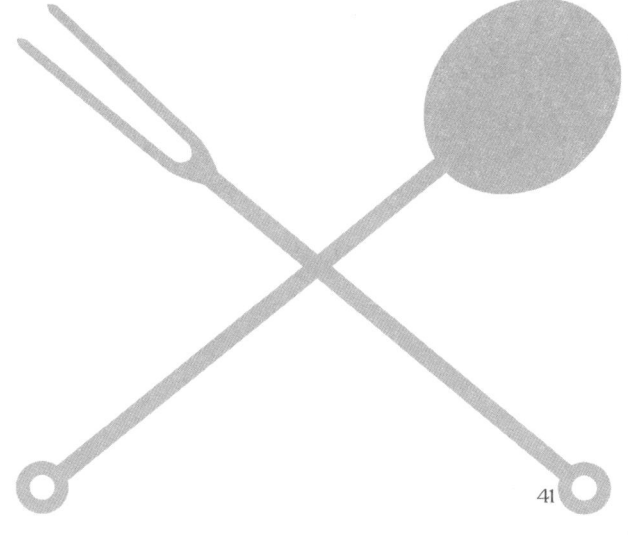

14
TEMPERANCE

Arcanum: 14
Zodiac Affinity: Sagittarius

A boatman stands at a dockside tavern. He is wearing an apron and has assumed the role of bartender. Wineglasses sway in the racks above his head and boats float gently on the water behind him. He is standing tall amidst the reeds. One bare leg is in the water, and the other is bent with his foot placed firmly on the side of his boat.

The Temperance Angel (for this is who he is) is staring straight ahead. He is holding a blue pitcher horizontally, and the cold water flows out and downwards. He is holding a red bottle vertically, and the wine is being blown towards the water. They connect in the bottom of a transparent goblet to form an infinity symbol that is made up of neither wine nor water, but something completely different. The light has cast shadows that evenly divide him into a creature of light on one side and dark on the other. The folds and creases of his apron perfectly echo the curves of the water and the boats that lie behind him. He is a visual metaphor, describing the magic of alchemy and transformation.

KEY ELEMENTS

Water and Wine: Water has long been associated with the feminine and the unconscious, and is a symbol of a life-giving force. Red wine is associated with blood, not just because of its color, but due to Biblical connotations, such as *drinking the blood of Christ* during Holy Communion. The spilling of red wine has become synonymous with sacrifice of some kind. The blending of water and wine describes the creation of a new life. It is a metaphor for transformation and rebirth.

Boats: Because of their connection with water, boats serve to describe an emotional state. They symbolize both a physical and a spiritual journey. In this card, the boats are empty and still. They represent vessels waiting to be filled, or transformed. A boat represents transition because it literally takes you from one place to another. In this card, it is about moving from one life phase to another by keeping an even keel.

Card Meaning

Two alchemical opposites, heat and cold, are used to temper metal or to change its form. First, the steel is melted by fire and then the liquid dross is molded and cooled into its new shape. The significance of this is the meaning behind the Temperance card. The old fashioned phrase, "to temper our mettle" means to find moderation in life, and this usually occurs as you balance what you want against what you need.

The Temperance card acknowledges that there are oppositional forces that co-exist within us all. Sagittarius is closely related to this card because the Archer is a Centaur—half-man, half-horse. It represents the merging of man and beast into something unique yet recognizable.

When you draw this card in a reading you are being asked to consider the chemistry of a situation. There are usually two or more opposing forces at play. This card is not about submission or giving in as Sagittarius the Archer aims his arrow high, but rather it is about finding the road to success through the perfect blending of elements. You need to blend desire with need, skill with task, emotion with action. The Temperance card suggests that walking the middle ground is the answer to restoring equilibrium amongst body, mind, and spirit. If one considers an uneven terrain, the middle road is the most efficient and direct route as time and energy can be wasted scaling mountain peaks and crawling through trenches.

Kitchen Wisdom

In cooking, there are five separate elements of flavor —sweet, sour, salty, bitter, and pungent. A chef knows how to blend these as like increases like, and opposites balance each other.

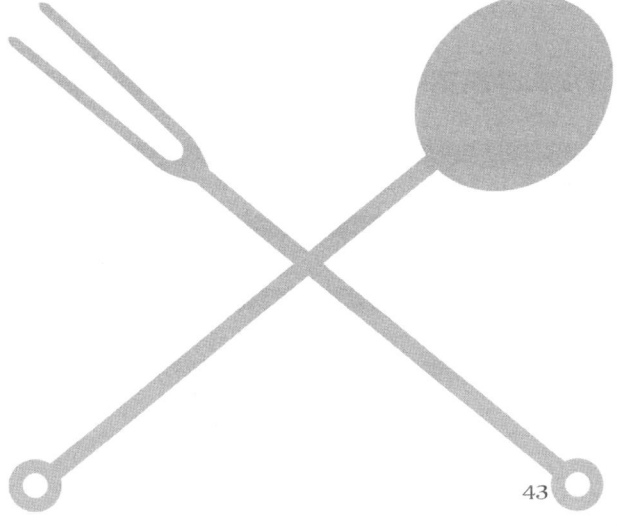

15 The Devil

Arcanum: 15
Zodiac Affinity: Capricorn

There is a nightmarish quality to this card. The Devil, half-man, half-goat, reclines on top of the refrigerator. He is wearing a mask, and with one hand, he rests a can of beer on top of his rounded belly. With his other hand, he reaches out, offering a slice of cake to the two humans in the foreground. They are wearing large golden chains that are attached to the doors of the same appliance that The Devil is resting on. They thrash around, pushing and pulling away from the cake. Smoke swirls around, and wine pours itself into a floating glass. It takes no stretch of the imagination to see that the two chained victims are being tempted by forbidden food and drink. It seems to be an overly dramatic reaction to the idea of dieting and self-restraint.

Key Elements

Devil: The Devil is traditionally known as a symbol of evil, the master of temptation and hedonistic desire. The Christian devil was the archangel Lucifer who fell from heaven because of his wild and uncontrollable behavior. The Devil of this card is more in line with Pan, or Bacchus, the god who is half-goat, in keeping with Capricorn, the goat figure of the zodiac. Capricorn is an earth sign that is associated with physical pleasure and material success. The goat, a symbol for Capricorn, is the one that strives to get to the top of the mountain peak. He claims power as his natural right—and that is hard to resist. It is well known that power is an aphrodisiac for many. The Devil aspect of the goat is in his unrestrained abandon; the unapologetic pleasure he takes in physical excess. The Devil itself is not evil, but rather is a symbol for the baser nature of man.

Chains: Chains are symbols for enslavement, bondage, and restriction. They represent a physical attachment to anything that is detrimental to good mental, physical, or emotional health. In this card, the chains are loosely worn, meaning that they can be slipped out of at any time. This implies that they are self-inflicted. They are representations of an Ego that has become obsessed with a desire for gratification.

CARD MEANING

The Devil in this card is strictly a man-made construction. There is no evil being or goat lurking in your kitchen, waiting to enslave an unsuspecting victim. The Devil is a product of the ego that wants more, more, more. The desire for power and pleasure is not necessarily a bad thing. The advancement of civilization by science, by the creation of art, music, and great culinary achievements were not made by people who were satisfied with mediocrity or were lacking in ambition. The trouble that we get into occurs when the desire for power and pleasure become overwhelming, and the effort that it takes to feed the desire becomes an addiction. We are then the slaves to our needs and The Devil has us in its grip.

When you draw this card in a reading, it is time to look at what sort of addictions are present in your life. Power, food, drugs, alcohol, sex, or material concerns all can play a role in self-bondage. If you can partake of these pleasures and feel guilt free and unapologetic, you are doing well. If you are so consumed by these needs that they are creating a lifestyle that is causing pain to yourself or others, then it is time to pay attention to The Devil.

The shadow side to The Devil is too much restraint. You feel unable to free yourself and feel moments of abandon. That is also a form of enslavement.

KITCHEN WISDOM

"If you get down and quarrel everyday,
you're saying prayers to the devil, I say."
~Bob Marley

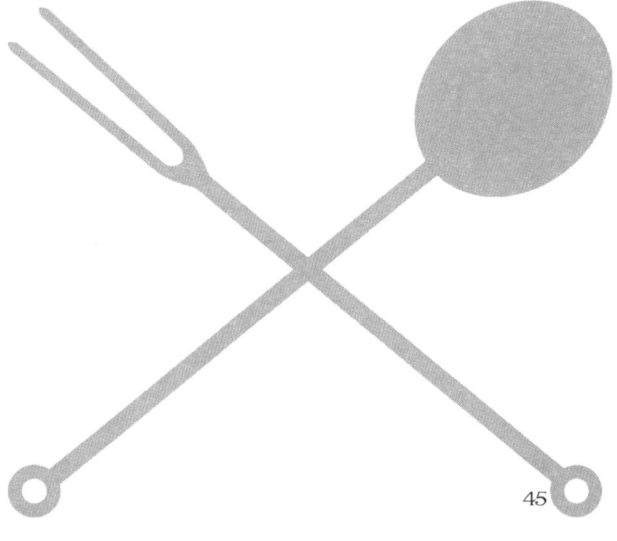

16 The Tower

Arcanum: 16
Zodiac Affinity: Mars

This scene shows disaster in the kitchen. The sink is full of dirty pots and utensils, and the soapy water is overflowing. There is a tower of dishes tilting sideways as if ready to topple over. A dog is in the act of stealing a turkey, pulling the tablecloth towards him, causing glasses to fall over and spilling their contents. In the background, a person carrying a multi-tiered cake has tripped and fallen, spilling the layers all over the floor. In traditional decks, The Tower is the only man-made structure depicted in the cards. In this case, it is a situation that has been totally crafted by man and beast.

Key Elements

Dishes: They represent how we receive emotional nourishment. According to dream dictionaries, the state of the dishes is significant to the state of our psyches. Dirty dishes represent both financial difficulties and obstacles in achieving our plans. To dream of dirty dishes stacked up, means that we are dreading the work that is in front of us in reality. Broken or damaged dishes are seen as forerunners to family quarrels or domestic problems. In the same light, unwashed dishes represent dissatisfaction and an unpromising outlook.

Falling: A fall represents a loss of control over some sort of situation. It implies that something is either unstable or needs to be fixed.

Card Meaning

The general feeling of this card is that of chaos. A lot of hard work that has utilized a great many resources has been destroyed by seemingly random acts. The turkey and the lavish cake were to be key items in an important dinner and they are no longer available at this, the eleventh hour of the presentation.

Mars, the Roman god of war, is closely related to The Tower card. His aggressive energy often signifies catastrophe. The message in this card is not subtle. All your careful plans and structured defense systems have been assaulted. Your physical, financial, and emotional well-being have come under attack. You have had no warning and no time to prepare for this sudden and devastating change of events that seems to have come out of the blue.

This seems like a terrible card to get in a reading. No one wants or welcomes chaos, but still it happens. Life has a way of shifting and changing despite all your attempts to keep things under control.

When you draw this card in a reading, it is generally viewed as an opportunity to start over. The kitchen disaster can be cleaned up. The guests can eat something else, and, in the long run, the catastrophe will be the makings of a very funny story. The key to this card is not the disaster itself, but the reaction to it.

The Tower card usually implies that there is a need to build a stronger foundation, one that will not be so easily knocked over. This can be seen most often in your attitude towards the unexpected. Do you *go with the flow* or do you rail against the inevitable?

The Tower is about having the strength to withstand an assault, and to be able to look back and see the situation as a gift rather than a curse.

The shadow side to this card lies in not seeing the opportunity to rebuild and refusing to move forward, preferring instead to wallow in misery and self-pity.

Kitchen Wisdom

When The Tower strikes and the power goes out,
you can either get a flashlight
or have some fun in the dark.

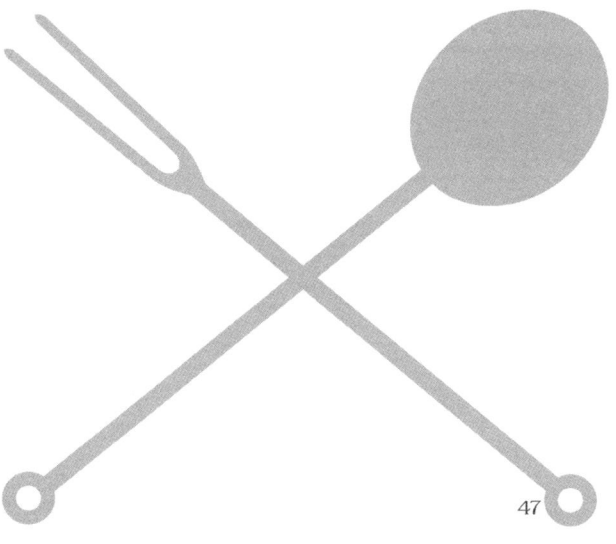

17 THE STAR

Arcanum: 17
Zodiac Affinity: Aquarius

This is a very non-traditional approach to The Star, the Tarot deck's *card of hope and truth*. A young woman is relaxing in the bathtub. Water is flowing from an open tap, creating small waves and bubbles all around her. She has a dreamy expression on her face as more water slips through her fingers and onto the floor. The curtain beside her is patterned with birds in flight and it is drawn back to reveal a small table. On the table is a cupcake with a sparkler stuck in the icing. The sparkler is lit and merrily blazing away, reminiscent of the night sky in Van Gogh's painting, *Starry Night*. It is a scene of peace and tranquility, a breath of fresh air following the tumult of The Tower.

KEY ELEMENTS

Female Figure: This young woman represents the archetype of youth and beauty. She is naked, discovered in the act of bathing. She is literally immersed in water, symbolizing purification, a washing away of troubles and cares. Nudity in Tarot symbolism often represents purity, innocence, and a lack of fear of exposure. This woman remains nude and is surrounded by the life-giving forces of water. She might not be totally innocent, but she is able to cleanse the past and enjoy the present.

Running Water: The unique property of water is that it has no form of its own, but rather borrows its shape from what it surrounds. Water follows the force of gravity, running from higher levels to lower ones. It is passive by nature and is affected by many influences. In this card, water is being actively channeled from the tap and into the bath, and it passively flows out through open fingers and onto the floor. This means that some of life's events we can do nothing about; external forces beyond our control can cause troubled waters. We can, however, redirect the flow. We can heal, rejuvenate, and again achieve wholeness through the miracle of optimism.

CUPCAKE WITH SPARKLER: This invokes childhood memories, times of joy and innocence. The light from the sparkler is dazzling, yet impractical for serious navigation. It is enough to enjoy the moment and not worry about what will happen when it goes out.

CARD MEANING

This card is about discovering one's own inner light, or guiding force. It acknowledges that troubled times have passed and that it is now time to rejuvenate and refresh both the body and the soul. It is time to breathe a metaphorical sigh of relief. There is no action that is required other than to be optimistic about the future. Enjoy a moment of well-deserved peace and harmony.

The shadow side to this card lies in being both arrogant and impractical, as in setting one's sights higher than one's capabilities—much like the little sparkler thinking it can light a stadium.

KITCHEN WISDOM

"Catch a falling star and put it in your pocket, save it for a rainy day..."
~Childhood nursery rhyme that still rings true

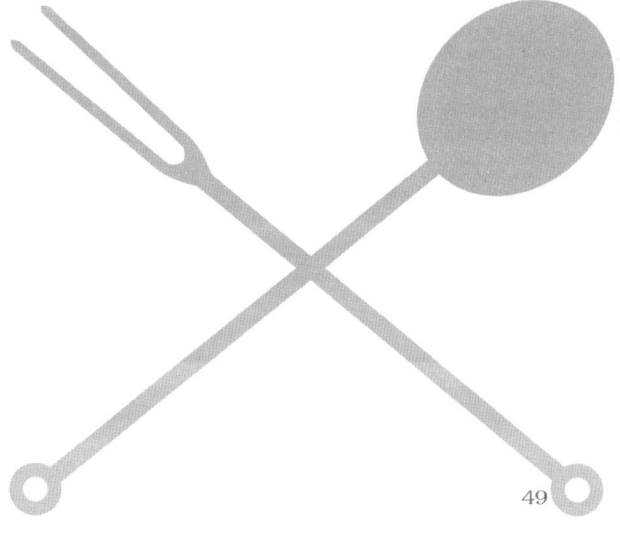

18 THE MOON

Arcanum: 18
Zodiac Affinity: Pisces

It is midnight, and a full moon is shining through the kitchen window. The light reflects off a bowl filled with harmless utensils creating a distorted, monster-like shadow on the table. As its huge claw reaches out, getting bigger by the moment, a large dog jumps up on a chair and begins to bark as if warding off attack. Her coat, normally a tawny gold, shines white in the crazy light. The beagle begins to howl. He has woken from a dream of digging up hidden treats and is more frightened than defensive. The black cat stretches, reaches up, and swats at the shadow, intrigued by this new development that has caused such havoc in the household.

KEY ELEMENTS

Dogs: The large barking dog and the small howling one are shown together to represent two extremes of reaction. The full moon exerts a powerful influence on our psyches. It brings out a desire for wildness and excess, as both passion and fear can leap out of control. The large dog represents a primal or attack reaction. It faces the challenge with a wild desire to join in. The little dog is more fearful and domesticated and is that nagging voice of conscience that shows restraint and control. Together, these dogs symbolize the struggle, or battle, that occurs in our minds when we feel the tug of the moon; they are reflections of internal chaos.

Cat: The household cat is a tamer and domesticated version of the lion, and represents strength and passion. In this card, the cat's reaction to a perceived threat is playful and curious. It symbolizes a lack of fear when dealing with the unknown. This willingness to explore the shadows is due to an extremely well-developed night vision.

Shadow: The distortion of kitchen implements into a scary lobster-like shadow suggests that we are not comfortable with our primal selves. Symbolically, the lobster, or crayfish, represents a primordial state of consciousness. It is basic and hidden, a part of the great unknown in our genetic makeup. The inner self can be either tapped or ignored. The path that we choose depends on our reaction to that shadow.

CARD MEANING

The Moon is associated with the zodiac sign of Pisces, which is represented by two fish swimming in opposite directions. This defines the meaning of the card. Pisces is the sign of the Visionary and speaks to both howling confusion and intense clarity. This is the card of both madness and genius, which come from the same deep wellspring of consciousness.

The Moon is a reflective surface, and in Tarot, what is reflected is the dark, or shadow side of the human psyche. When you draw this card in a reading, it is your reaction to the shadows that determines the outcome. It can signify a time of great creativity or a period of utter confusion. If there are tendencies towards alcoholism, depression or any mental illness, the tug of the moon will pull you towards that downward path. The key to dealing with the effects of The Moon is to recognize the struggle and to channel the energy into positive actions. The middle ground is the safest path; it does not bring extremes. If you are not prepared to embark on a creative project, stay away from the negative influences.

KITCHEN WISDOM

We are our choices. We can choose idle hands
and an overactive imagination, or busy hands and a creative mind.

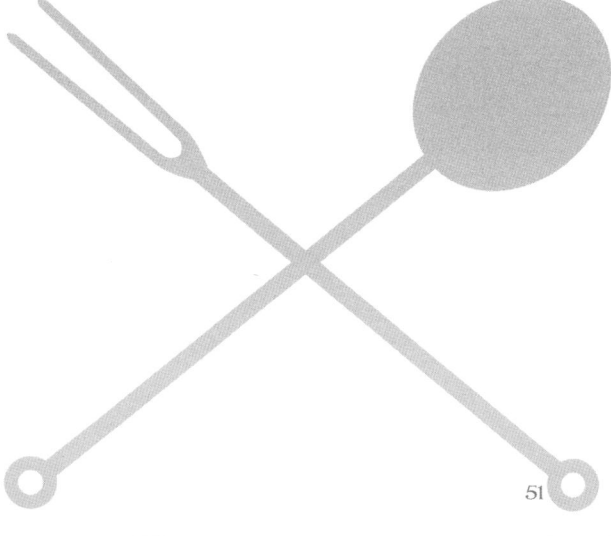

19 THE SUN

Arcanum: 19
Zodiac Affinity: The Sun

It is a beautiful day, the sun is shining, and soft breezes are blowing. Perfect weather for a picnic at the beach. You can hear the laughter from this happy toddler as he delights in the scene. His arms are partially outstretched as if he is unable to decide between wanting to be picked up and wanting to grab one of the sunflowers in the vase. The adults are not visible, although they are very close by busily laying out the food and spreading more blankets. In the background, the sea is calm and the waves gently brush against the shore. On the radio, an oldies station is playing "Here Comes the Sun," and everyone agrees with The Beatles that it has indeed been a "long, cold, lonely winter." But, it is clearly over now. Time to have some fun.

KEY ELEMENTS

Baby: In a reading, a baby could symbolize a pregnancy, but does not necessarily hold that specific meaning. Infants also impart feelings of innocence and the purity of childhood. They speak to the inner child and are often an invitation to give up one's cares and worries, or even a daily routine, in order to come outside and play. A baby is also a fragile creature that requires nurturing and constant attention and implies a need to be careful.

Sunflowers: They belong to the genus *Helianthus* and are a reference to Helios, the sun god. They represent adoration, longevity, warmth, and happiness. As they grow, sunflowers turn their faces towards the sun and therefore symbolize the sun itself.

Orange: Orange can either be a fruit or a color. As a color, it represents the second chakra, which is located near the womb and is associated with creativity. Orange combines the energy of red with the happiness of yellow. It is the color associated with autumn, optimism, and vitality. As a fruit, an orange tree is a symbol of love. In Chinese food symbolism, an orange represents luck and good fortune, especially when eaten on the second day of a New Year.

Eggs: They represent fertility, rebirth, and the cycle of life. In Christian religions, eggs are served at Easter as a symbol of the resurrection. In Jewish religions, eggs are placed on the Seder plate as part of the Passover tradition. They symbolize sacrifice and loss. In China, a red egg is given out at the one-month birthday of a new baby to celebrate fertility and the beginning of life.

Card Meaning

This is the most optimistic card of a Tarot deck. It implies that a time of hardship and struggle is over, and a period of prosperity and happiness has begun. The sun is the life force of the solar system, and we are illuminated by its rays and filled with insight and clarity. When you draw this card in a reading, it means that it is time to recharge your batteries and gain a new vitality. This is the time when good things will happen with very little effort on your part. The Sun card asks that you believe in the benevolence of the universe and live in the secure knowledge that you will be provided with what you need. It is possible to achieve a state of grace when you can accept good fortune and count your blessings.

The shadow side to this card is very mild. You could compare it to a slight sunburn. The joy is present, but just to a lesser degree. That is still a pretty good deal. So, go on, take a break, go outside and play.

Kitchen Wisdom

"Sun, sun, sun, here it comes…"
~ The Beatles. Lyrics from "Here comes the Sun."

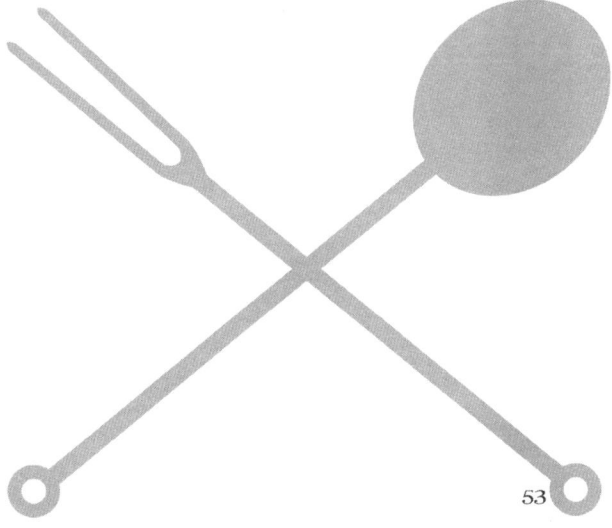

20
Judgment

Arcanum: 20
Zodiac Affinity: Pluto

This card was inspired by the destruction of the city of New Orleans in the wake of hurricane Katrina. It is a tribute to the subsequent rebuilding of a city and the resurrection of its culture and cuisine. Despite the non-traditional imagery (no naked people rising from open graves to heed the angel's call), this card holds true to its original meaning and intention.

A woman is smiling as she holds up a decorated cake. She is being handed a blue ribbon by a man wearing a suit, presumably the judge. In the background, the curtains part and a trumpet player blasts his music towards the spotlight. The mood is joyous and celebratory.

Key Elements

Blue Ribbon: The original Blue Ribbon, or *Cordon Bleu*, was given as the highest order of chivalry to certain knights by the Bourbon kings. The next historical Blue Ribbon came from *Blue Riband* and was the prize given to the fastest ship that crossed the Atlantic. It has come to be associated with first place, and is a symbol for something of high value. Traditionally, a bride is to wear something borrowed and something blue, as a blue ribbon represents fidelity.

Cake: A cake is a symbol of celebration. There are many kinds for all occasions. In Biblical times, the bread of cakes was distinguished from common bread, as the former implied love toward a neighbor, and common bread had a more celestial meaning. Today, the term, "piece of cake" refers to a straightforward task that is easily accomplished.

Trumpet: A trumpet is one of the oldest instruments. It is used even now in military fanfare as a call to assemble, or a command to march. In symbolic terms a trumpet call heralds new life triumphing over death. In Tarot decks, a trumpet blast is an audible call to rise out of complacency. It is a calling for an awakening of our higher selves.

CARD MEANING

The zodiac affinity for the Judgment card is Pluto. It is the planet furthest away from the earth, and is associated with the god of the underworld, rebirth, and illumination. (In this deck, though there is scientific evidence that Pluto is not a planet, it will still be treated as such in *The Cook's Tarot*.) This is a very personal card that involves making final important decisions about leaving the past behind and moving forward. It signifies healing, acceptance and the ability to judge without condemning.

When you draw this card in a reading, you are being given a second chance. It means that you can look back on past mistakes and come to terms with them. You can examine past scenarios, even those involving horror and abuse, and move forward into a state of grace. It takes an epiphany of the soul to be able to forgive—both others and yourself—but this is necessary, as there is no benefit to self-victimization and no progress in hatred.

This feeling of guilt and blame represents the shadow side to this card and signifies an inability to move forward.

KITCHEN WISDOM

Liberate yourself from old habits by throwing out everything that does not fit with who you want to be. Don't look back.

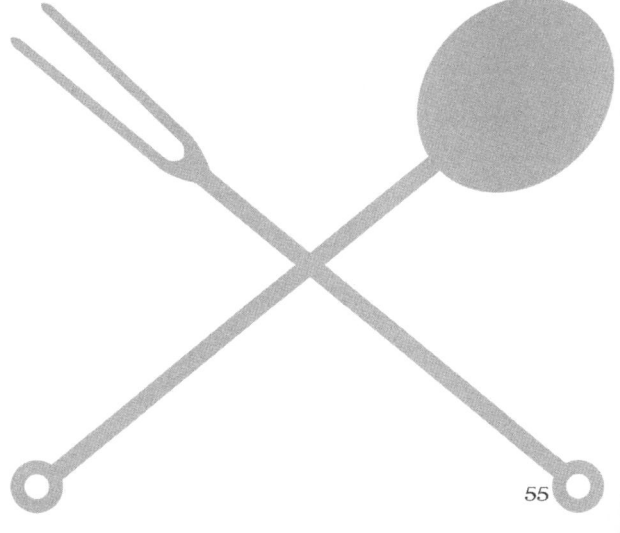

21 THE WORLD

Arcanum: 21
Zodiac Affinity: Saturn

THE WORLD

The theme of this card is, "The world is your oyster." This British colloquialism has its origins in Shakespeare, specifically: Act II, Scene 1 of *The Merry Wives of Windsor*.

> **Falstaff:** I will not lend thee money.
> **Pistol:** Why, then, the world's mine oyster, which I with sword shall open.

It has come to mean that the world is yours for the taking, it is a place to extract easy success and profit. It is what you make of it.

The young woman in this card has her bags packed and waiting at her feet. She raises a final glass in toast to all those who have made the journey possible. She is shown behind a map of the world that has the coordinates for latitude and longitude along its borders. A large open oyster shell is superimposed on top of the map. A pearl necklace is curled inside and spills out, encircling the globe in a loosely formed lemniscate.

KEY ELEMENTS

Pearl: As one of the oldest known gemstones, the history of the pearl is rich with magic and folklore. Early cultures believed that a single drop of rain fell from the heavens and became the heart of an oyster. Pearls are also known as *teardrops of the moon* as they are strongly associated with female, water, and Lunar cycles. Pearls have come to symbolize the best within us: honesty, purity, innocence, concentration, and focus. Pearls strung on a thread represent order, and a pearl necklace is said to symbolize cosmic unity. The necklace is said to connect spiritual relationships between separate individuals or scattered elements.

Woman's Posture: Traditionally, the figure in The World card is shown as a dancer with one leg bent in an upright version of The Hanged Man's posture. This is to show that she is no longer inward seeking, but is now looking outward. In this card the dancer has become the traveler. The Fool has come to the end of one journey, and she has her bags packed and ready for the next. Her position signifies balance and symmetry as the bent arm corresponds to the bent leg, and the straight leg, firmly planted on the ground compliments the arm, extending upward, raised in a toast.

Card Meaning

The World is the last card of the Major Arcana. It is closely related to the planet Saturn, one of the oldest in the zodiac. Saturn is known as the Teacher, the Great Tester, and also the Bringer of Sorrow. Individuals learn lessons through patience and discipline only after they have abandoned all ideas that are not based on a realistic perception of the material conditions of life. In other words, The World card represents self-knowledge that has been hard won. You have not only survived, but have triumphed over the challenges.

This is a card of wholeness. A card in which everything comes together as body, mind, and spirit and are integrated. We finally feel connected and aware of our happiness. When you draw this card in a reading, it is a very positive sign. It can mean one of three things. First, there is the sense of completion, as whatever you have been working towards will be achieved. Second, there is the expectation of things shifting to the next level, as in a student becoming the teacher. And third, there is the idea of a journey of significance, either by actual travel or by embarking on a new spiritual course.

The shadow side to this card comes with finding your world too small. You might feel stuck in a tedious situation, or be unwilling to step outside your comfort zone. In this case, you have many more lessons to learn.

Kitchen Wisdom

Cycles are funny things: some of them even come with wheels and an engine.

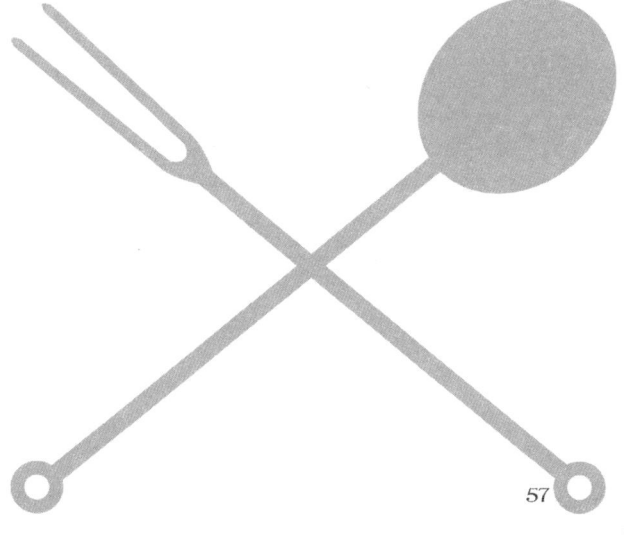

The Minor Arcana

The Minor Arcana are the 58 cards of the Tarot deck that deal with the everyday or commonplace occurrences of daily life. The insight that we gain, and the choices or options in our response to them are based on their position in a "layout" or "spread." An easy way to relate to the Minor Arcana is to think of them as four different families living in the same neighborhood. Each family, or suit of cards, will have a different reaction to similar situations based on their personalities or elemental association.

Each family, or suit, is represented by its Court Cards: the King, Queen, Knight, and Page. They can be thought of as Father (ruler King), Mother (diplomat Queen), Teenager (volatile Knight), and Child (innocent Page). Even though these cards are traditionally gender and age specific, *The Cook's Tarot* recognizes that the spirit inherent in each role can be applied to anyone at any time in life.

Wands

The family, or suit, of Wands is associated with the element of fire. It corresponds to such things as passion, energy, creativity, and often is related to career choices. The Wand's persona is very capable; they are high achievers and often ego-driven. This suit is about getting things done and represents external values.

Cups

The family, or suit, of Cups is associated with the element of water. Cups are considered to be the symbolic vessels that contain our emotions. They correspond to both our conscious and unconscious desires and how we relate to others on a daily basis. The Cup's persona will trust their hearts over their heads when making a decision. They are very comfortable with their internal barometers and are good at empathizing with spiritual and emotional issues.

Swords

The family, or suit, of Swords is associated with the element of air. This corresponds to mental energy, or the way in which we think about things. This suit advocates a logical, rather than emotional approach to problem solving. They will trust their heads over their hearts when making a decision. As swords are double edged, this family tends to learn its lessons the hard way.

Pentacles

The family, or suit, of Pentacles is associated with the element of earth. This generates a strong grounding or stabilizing energy. This persona is practical and hard-working. They are concerned with such things as finances, material possessions that will provide creature comforts, health, and sensuality.

Each suit contains a set of Court Cards, an Ace (which sets the tone for the rest of the cards) and nine other cards numbered 2 to 10. The numerological meaning of each card is discussed as part of its interpretation or card meaning.

Ace of Wands

This image is an interpretation of the phrase, "spark of creativity." There is a lot happening in this card. The foreground is dominated by a large hand that is performing an act of transformation. An oak leaf is held firmly between two fingers, and as the pressure increases, the stem becomes an incendiary that bursts into flame as it comes into contact with a matchbox cover. There are various combinations of matches and leaves falling to the ground, as if the previous attempts at magic were not as successful.

All this action is taking place in front of a stove that has its oven door wide open. The heat is radiating out, and the steam from a cake that is baking on a rack inside mingles with the flame of the match.

In the background is a tiny castle casting its long shadow on the colorfully checkered floor. There is a sense of unreality, tension, and excitement. Our senses are on high alert as we can hear the snap and hiss of the match, feel the heat and steam from the oven, and smell the tempting aromas that are wafting outwards.

Key Elements

Flame: The Wand suit is associated with the element of fire. It represents energy, passion, and creativity. In this card, a match has just burst into flame, meaning that an idea has just materialized. It is that flash of brilliance, the creative spark, that marks the beginning of a new adventure. The discovery of fire was primal to the advancement of civilization and it also plays a key role in its destruction. The very nature of fire is that it is dangerous if left untended, yet essential if its powers are channeled and guided.

Oak Leaf: Just as the lion is king of the jungle, the oak tree is considered king of the forest. The oak leaf symbolizes strength, endurance, and longevity. The meaning in this card is that the flame of an idea needs the strength and endurance of an oak to carry it to fruition.

Castle: It is a fortress to be defended, and often the destination point of a long and arduous quest.

CARD MEANING

All of the aces symbolize new beginnings. The disembodied hands that appear in traditional decks seem to imply that what is offered in that hand is not attached to the rest of the body. In other words, it is a brief, fleeting gift with no history or expectations attached to it. What you make of it is entirely up to you. The Ace of Wands is that spark of creativity that seems to come out of nowhere. It can just as easily fizzle out and amount to nothing if you ignore it. Ideas are easy—everyone has millions of them. It is the ability to recognize potential and also to act on it that separates the individual from the herd.

When you draw this card in a reading, it means that it is time to act on an inspiration. Bring all the fire and passion that The Wands have to offer by believing in your idea. Realize that the journey must begin somewhere, and it might as well begin now.

The shadow side of this card is that you might be burned by your idea, because you did not control its direction. Employ the strength of the oak tree and have patience once the initial creative flare has diminished. Ideas by themselves mean nothing. It takes hard work to make them a reality.

KITCHEN WISDOM

A good idea is a new career waiting to happen.

Two of Wands

A figure wearing a jaunty red hat, glasses, and a cape is standing still. He seems poised between action and thought. He is holding an unlit candle in one hand and a box of matches in the other. Directly in front of him is an elaborately decorated cake with a single candle perched on top. Its flame is giving off a trail of smoke that wafts through the air and out the open window. The young man is torn. There is an empty pan waiting to be filled sitting on the table beside the cake that he has completed, yet his gaze wanders to the view outside and towards the lure of the globe that is perched on the window ledge.

Key Elements

Candle: The symbolic meaning of a candle is dependent on the context in which it is shown. A birthday candle has a different intention from one that is used in religious ceremonies or pagan rituals. However, a feature that they all have in common is that a candle, in order to fulfill itself, must burn itself out. A candle that is never lit will never fulfill its purpose, which could be to provide a spark of joy, to simply light the dark, or to symbolize an act as a prayer. A candle that is lit symbolizes intellect, enlightenment, awareness, and a search for the truth. A candle that is unlit symbolizes rejection, disappointment, and not utilizing one's full potential.

Globe: In one sense, a globe can symbolize travel and a sense of adventure. In a broader sense, it takes on further meaning such as *having a global view* or a wider perspective on things. A spinning globe is symbolic of life that is out of control.

Card Meaning

The 2 of Wands is about making a decision about which creative path to follow. The spark that was evident in The Ace of Wands has come to fruition and success has been obtained. The choice is to continue along these same lines and increase the potential for even more growth, or to do something different and veer off in a new direction.

Because the suit of Wands is associated with the element of fire, it speaks to ambition as well as passion. The number 2 is about balance and union, but it is also about duality, and this is where the choice is required. In matters of career choices, or any creative endeavor, you have to decide if you want to double your profits with a sure bet or to seize the day by grasping a fresh opportunity.

When you draw this card in a reading, you are probably feeling a bit indecisive and unsure about what to do next. What do you see when you look at the card? Do you see a candle that is waiting to join its mate? Or, do you see it sitting on a second cake? Or are you already out the door, heading for the distant horizon? In this case, you have another choice. Either wait to see what presents itself or follow your heart.

The shadow side to this card lies in perpetual indecision, and an inability to move forward.

Kitchen Wisdom

You can't burn a candle at both ends and expect to have it last very long.

Three of Wands

High on top of a windy cliff, a young man tends his fire while looking out over the ocean. He has created a balanced tripod with his body, as he is in a runner's position, using both feet and one arm for support. With his free arm he is holding a fork that he has fashioned out of a slender tree branch and is calmly roasting marshmallows. The smoke from his campfire is rising up and forming puffy cloud signals. They catch the breeze and head out towards a ship just cresting the horizon. There is a sense of active waiting in this scene, as the smoke beckons the ship forward, and the young man looks ready to spring into action at any moment.

Key Elements

Fire: The element associated with the suit of Wands. It is a symbol of creativity, passion, adventure, and ambition. In this card, fire is the catalyst for success. It is responsible for creating the signals that draw the ship forward.

Compass: An open compass lies on the ground beside the campfire. The original compasses were developed in order to study the heavens, or "celestial canopy." The result was to bring people closer to thinking of God as the supreme architect of the universe. It has since come to symbolize the spiritual or higher nature of humankind. In this card, the compass has both practical and symbolic applications. It reminds us that it is important to know the route before starting on a journey.

Oak Leaf: Beside the compass there is a single oak leaf resting on the ground, half in shadow. An oak tree symbolizes courage and strength, especially in the face of adversity, "out of a single acorn, a mighty oak tree grows." A single leaf, however, represents happiness. This card suggests that personal fulfillment lies in the strength found in self-confidence and the ability to trust one's intuition, or internal compass.

Ship: Water represents unconscious desires or emotions. A ship, because it sails on water, is synonymous with life's journey. The state of the surrounding water and the position of the ship serve to describe the hidden desires that lie within this card. This particular ship is coming *full steam ahead* towards shore. The water is deep, but not particularly turbulent. Success is close to hand, but it takes creative solutions to guide the ship home.

CARD MEANING

The Three of Wands, like all the Tarot threes, is about branching out. This card speaks to the start of a new and successful adventure. The allegorical ship has not yet arrived, but the creative powers are already at work bringing it closer.

When you draw this card in a reading, you are being asked to consider moving in a new direction. It is not a card of impulsive action, but rather one of foresight and planning. You are being asked to consider where you fit in the big picture. It is time to think outside the proverbial box because it will take creative solutions to overcome the inertia of the status quo.

The shadow side of this card lies both in an inability to move forward due to over-planning, or on the opposite spectrum, in moving too quickly without considering the consequences of your actions. The solution to this dilemma involves a balancing act between the courage to start something new and the patience to plan the proper course of action.

KITCHEN WISDOM

It is better to watch a ship coming towards you, than to watch it going away.

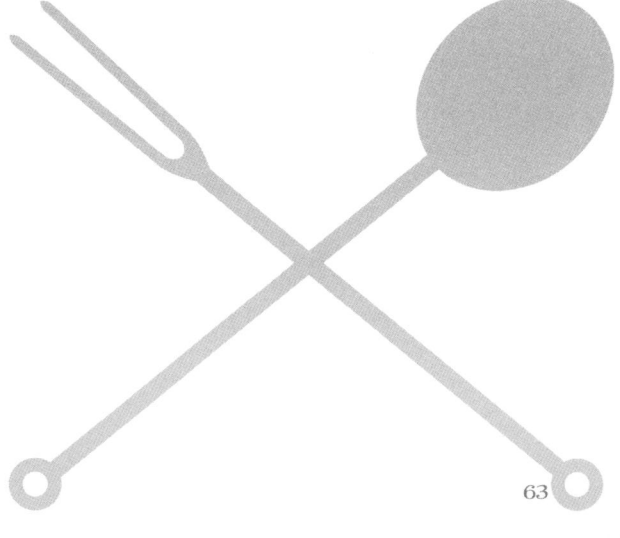

Four of Wands

This is a time of celebration. The young couple are getting ready for their wedding ceremony, the groom has torn a piece of bread from one of the four loaves and is feeding it to his future bride. Roses, grapes, and oak leaves circle the wicker basket on the table. This couple is about to walk through the archway and begin a new life together. A kite is seen in the background, dancing merrily in the cloudless blue sky.

Key Elements

Bread: Throughout the world, bread has always been one of the staple elements of any diet. In biblical times, it was associated with the body, and more particularly, the body of Christ. To *break bread* is also a longstanding tradition implying socialization and community. In days before the invention of cutlery, bread was literally torn, or broken, by the hands and offered to others at the table. In this card, the four loaves of bread are a tribute to the earthly qualities found in the number 4. Four represents stability, as in the four sides to a square, the four seasons, the four directions, the four winds, and so on.

The Couple: The Four of Wands is about joyous commitment to a person or venture. The marriage ceremony celebrates the union of two people. They have gone beyond the initial phases of liking and choosing, and are now creating a solid foundation for the rest of their lives. The roses, grapes, oak leaves, and even the long hair of the bride are all symbols of prosperity and abundance.

Archway: Literally an opening or a gateway, arches represent moving forward in a new direction. In this case it is a physical movement that signifies a change in mental attitude. Arches also convey a sense of protection for the people under them.

CARD MEANING

The Four of Wands is a happy card. The ship that was on the horizon in the Three of Wands has come in to port. It is a time of celebration and prosperity. Four corresponds with The Emperor card in the Major Arcana and shares with it some of the same qualities, such as an appreciation of material goods and a display of the traditional male roles involving authority and protection. However, the bride in this card has her hair undone and flowing loosely down her back. She is free of restraint and will be her own person.

When you draw this card in a reading, it is time to relax and enjoy a period of contentment. Wands symbolize fire energy and passion for creative ventures. In this card the energy is more inwardly directed and the creativity could involve the appearance of new family members. This is a good time to set up house, start a business, or begin any enterprise that will need to be based on a solid foundation.

The shadow side to this card is that you could be celebrating a little too much and ignoring some important things that need to get done.

KITCHEN WISDOM

You are now free to move around the cabin.
Get away from circumstances that don't suit you.

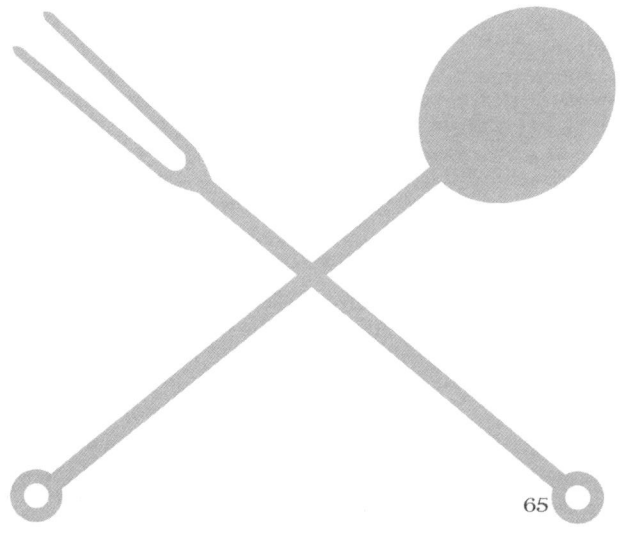

Five of Wands

FIVE OF WANDS

A group of five blindfolded individuals, wearing different colored shirts, are swinging their bats at a pinata. Each of them has a unique grip on their bats, and are approaching the prize from separate angles as they get ready to strike. The young people look as if they are enjoying themselves, although some are more intent on a victory than others. No one seems to have noticed that one of the decorated points has broken off, and candy is spilling onto the ground.

Key Elements

Pinata: There is some thought that the early Aztecs would fill clay pots with small treasures. They would decorate these pots with feathers and ceremoniously break them open with sticks as a tribute to the gods. As the treasures flowed out onto the ground, it was taken as a symbolic flow of abundance towards the people. In the sixteenth century, Spanish missionaries transformed this tradition to suit their own message. The clay pot became converted into a seven-pointed star. Each point symbolized a particular sin. The pinata was smashed in order to destroy sin. Today, the pinata is associated with birthdays and other festive celebrations.

Blindfold: A blindfold literally prevents one from seeing their surroundings. In a positive way, it has become a metaphor describing impartiality and acceptance, as in the phrases, "justice is blind" and "love is blind."

In a more negative way, a blindfold is symbolic of either a refusal to see clearly or of being victimized. The deciding factors would have to be who placed the blindfold and why?

Card Meaning

In this deck, the Five of Wands represents playful competition while learning to work together. None of the individuals in this card want all the candy for themselves. It is a foregone conclusion that all the proceeds will be shared. The challenge lies in who will be the first to break the piñata. The different colored shirts and the multiple ways of holding the bat represent cultural diversity and also individual differences within the same culture.

The blindfolds make the game more challenging and add an element of surprise to the proceedings. You could be swinging your bat in the right direction or you could be totally off course. In order to know where to direct your aim, you will have to listen to the others shouting and trust your instincts. It is obvious that if all the players took their blindfolds off, they could easily secure the prize, but that is not the point. There would be no fun in such an easy victory.

When you draw this card in a reading, you are being asked if there is a particular issue or situation that you are being "blind" to. Are you refusing to face certain facts or are you denying a particular reality? This card can also mean that you are being faced with multicultural challenges and you must learn or accept a different way of doing things. The 5 of Wands speaks to rivalry and disputes but not in a serious way. It is more about asserting yourself in order to come to terms with the group. Each must be respected for their individual skills.

The shadow side of this card is about being uncomfortable with asserting yourself. You would rather run from conflict, than have to face it. This can work, but there will not be any candy in your bag at the end of the party.

Kitchen Wisdom

Remember, you can always take off a blindfold.

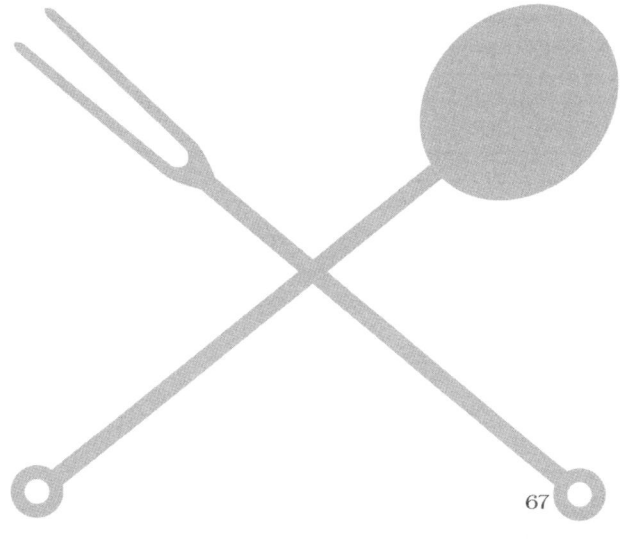

Six of Wands

Here is a moment of celebration for this young chef. She has won the cooking competition, and even the fish on the platter seems to be smiling and cheering her on. She raises both arms above her head in a time-honored gesture of triumph. The 6 wooden spoons that she waves proudly in the air are symbols of the tools of her trade that have now become symbols of her victory. The guests at the table are well dressed for this important occasion, and the surrounding orange painted walls seem to reflect their happiness. Their obvious support and approval make the pleasure of this moment even greater.

Key Elements

6 Wooden Spoons: The number 6 was considered by ancient mathematicians to be the perfect number. It has since come to mean many things, such as communication, harmony, and balance. Six is also considered to be lucky as it is the highest number on dice. The bees make their hives using a hexagon pattern, and 6 is strongly related to matters of home and family. In this card, the wooden spoons represent the six wands. These types of spoons are common to virtually every nation on earth. Symbolically, they represent ordinary life, or folk art. To dream of a wooden spoon indicates that there is a need to give or receive nourishment, and it could also mean that you feel that someone is getting special treatment. The Wooden Spoon Award has become known as a "booby prize" or mock award for those who finish last in a competition. It is ironic to use spoons in this card as a symbol of victory, but they speak to the cautionary aspect of the 6 of Wands, in that "pride often comes before fall."

Raised Arms: The chef is raising her arms above her head in the traditional "V" for victory position. Raising one's arms above the head makes the heart work harder as it has to pump blood against gravitational forces. It is a sign of cardiac fitness to be able to maintain this position, especially while holding weights. In this card, it is seen as a sign of ebullience and pride. It is a gesture, made by the naturally fit to symbolize triumph.

CARD MEANING

The Six of Wands symbolizes personal triumph that is earned by hard work and the completion of a difficult task. It speaks to a high point in regards to one's career, and it could also indicate that good news is about to be delivered.

This is a very positive card, in that you should take the time to bask in the glory of a well-earned success. It is also a cautionary card, in that success can also lead to a feeling of superiority, and a sense of triumph can evolve into unattractive gloating.

When you draw this card, you are being congratulated by the grand collective unconscious that you delve into with a Tarot reading. The universal forces are saying, "Well done, you." But, like all mysterious entities, these forces are also waiting to see what you will do next. They are, of course, hoping that you will display a little humility and acknowledge the help you had in obtaining your victory. They would also like you to be graceful in triumph and not to develop a taste for being the center of attention. If you disappoint them, you could be handed the Wooden Spoon Award.

KITCHEN WISDOM

"Judge your success by what you had to give up in order to get it."
~Dalai Lama XIV

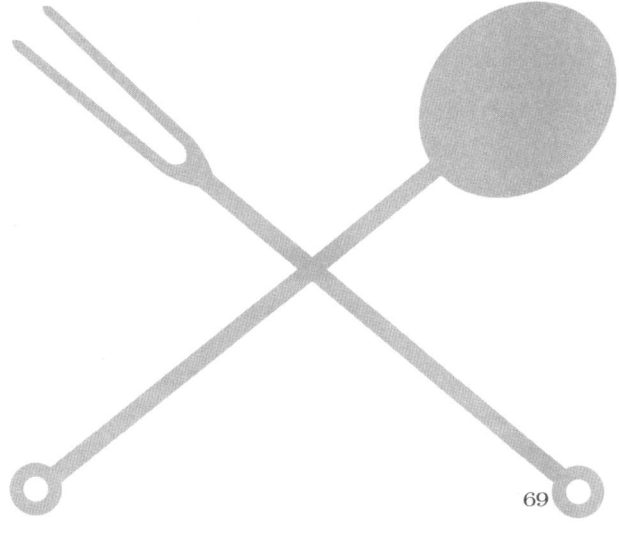

Seven of Wands

This scene is an illustration of two separate events that are occurring simultaneously. In the foreground, a mouse in his hole is barricading himself from the outstretched claws of a cat with a matchstick turned shovel. In the background, a man with a rolling pin is staving off the attack of what seems to be blackbirds that have flown out of a pie. Both parties feel that they are in danger, and have chosen whatever weapons they have close to hand, appropriate or not, to defend their positions.

There is no question that the mouse is in acute danger, but mice do not belong in kitchens. The cat is defending his territory, but is also looking forward to the thrill of the chase and an easy meal. The man is struggling with issues that could be real, but are most likely fictitious. The irony is that he could easily be catching the very real mouse in his kitchen. This scene addresses the age-old question: "Who is the victor and who is the victim?" Each of the characters involved would have a different answer.

Key Elements

Cat and Mouse: The cat-and-mouse game seems like a version of the childish pastime, hide-and-seek. The victor is the one who remains hidden by using imagination and trickery. In this instance, it is being used as a metaphor, describing both the valor and the foolishness of a heroic stand. We admire the mouse because, despite the fact that the odds are so clearly against him, he is being brave and standing up to his enemy. Victory in this case should have been obtained by retreat. The cat appears to be the aggressor, and a bit of a bully, but it is his job to rid the kitchen of thieving mice.

Blackbirds Baked in a Pie: This phrase is from an old English nursery rhyme, "Sing a Song of Sixpence." There is a record of live birds being placed in a pie for the amusement of sixteenth century nobility, but, in this case, the blackbirds represent black thoughts, or inner demons. They demonstrate an internal struggle that is often the result of paranoia and an overactive imagination. These thoughts can also be seen as the struggle of the ego as it strives for domination.

CARD MEANING

The Seven of Wands is about maintaining a defensive position against attacks that are either perceived or real. It is a card that asks you to consider what is involved in maintaining the upper hand. When you draw this card in a reading, there has usually been a preceding period of hard work and effort. This has been rewarded and you are now basking in the glow of success and approval. You are on top of the metaphorical heap. Often, when you think that you have something valuable, you feel that others want to take it from you. Enemies seem to appear and your position is now threatened.

Sometimes these threats are very real, and you have to take a stand and defend what you hold dear and believe in. There is no compromise or negotiation possible. You just have to recognize the difference between bravery and foolishness when you stand up to your convictions.

At other times, the effort to keep something important becomes a complicated struggle. It takes such a toll on you that in the end you wonder if the effort was worth it. The key to this card is to understand what you are fighting for and to accept the consequences.

The shadow side to a conflict situation is to avoid it for the wrong reasons, such as fear or cowardice. The opposite also exists, that instead of having a victim mentality and not believing that you have a right to succeed, you become the bully or aggressor in order to satisfy the demands of the ego. So many pitfalls!

KITCHEN WISDOM

There is no room for doubt in the middle of a battle.

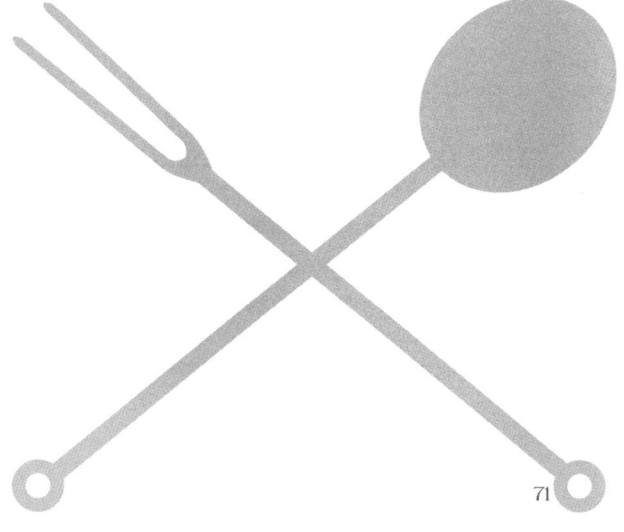

Eight of Wands

Eight oversized matches spiral down towards a table surrounded by eight empty chairs. There is a large birthday cake sitting on a colorful green tablecloth with eight candles circling its perimeter. There is a primitive, Stonehenge feel to the placement of the candles as they tilt and lean over the icing. An invitation that has been opened lies beside the cake. The room is dark and it is unclear as to whether people have just left, or if they have not yet arrived. The silence is profound.

Key Elements

Matches: The matchsticks symbolize the suit of Wands. They represent fire, energy, and passion. In this instance, they speak to an unrealized potential as they have not yet *caught fire*. It is interesting to note that the wands are not unidirectional as is often seen in more traditional interpretations. This is because life is not linear. This card implies that opportunities present themselves from all angles, and like a heat-seeking missile once the target is locked in sight the explosion will be significant.

Empty Chairs and Empty Tables: This is the title of a solo from the opera, *Les Miserables*, adapted from a book of the same name by Victor Hugo. The song occurs towards the end of the show when Marius mourns a place "where my friends will meet no more." It is full of regret and the futility of sacrifice.

The symbolism behind empty chairs is rather literal. One is not present. It implies an absence of awareness or motivation. In the *Dream Dictionary: A-Z Dream Meanings*, an empty chair signifies unexpected news.

Birthday Cake and Candles: The tradition of having a birthday cake dates back as far as ancient Greece. The offering to Artemis, goddess of the Moon, was a circular cake that had candles imbedded around it. When the candles were lit, the cake glowed like a full moon.

Candles have historically been used to send signals up to the gods who live in the sky. The act of making a wish and blowing out the candles would ensure that the message would be received and the wish would be granted. To this day, we honor that tradition.

CARD MEANING

The Eight of Wands is a card that tells you that the waiting is almost over. You will be receiving news and hopefully it will *light your fire*.

Since there is no specific direction to these wands, you cannot really tell the source of the news by the cards that surround it. Instead, you must choose what chair you decide to metaphorically sit in. They are all waiting and empty, so the choice is up to you. If you sit at the head of the table, then you will be the one opening the invitation—you will be in charge of a project or gathering. If it feels more comfortable to sit further back, then your news or your direction will take on a more philosophical and observational role.

The shadow side to this card is that you walk away and do not choose a chair. You are not ready to be "present" in life, or at the table. The news will not be recognized; the invitation will not be read.

KITCHEN WISDOM

Awareness is that moment when you "get it"
and you feel connected to the universe.
In other words, you know your place at the table.

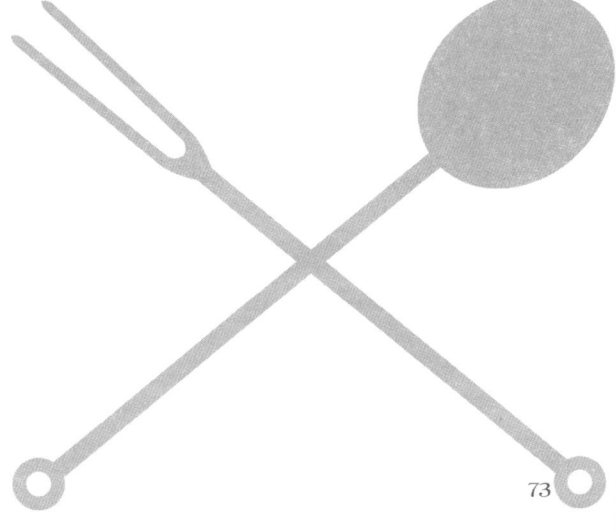

Nine of Wands

A man with a bemused expression on his face is surrounded by a nuisance of cats: one of them is leaping through the air towards him. In his right hand, he holds a tightly wrapped paper, or contract, out of its reach. With his other arm, he clutches a large cheese close to his body and away from the other would-be attackers.

Key Elements

Cats: They are the frequent subject of folklore and superstition and represent many contradictory qualities. They can be either the harbingers of good or bad luck. A cat's tail is thought to be the main indicator of its mood, and yet an upright tail can mean aggression in one situation and fear in another. Cats can be aloof and discerning, or curious and affectionate. No one really knows the mind of a cat, thus their reputation for mystery and inscrutability. The phrase "All cats are grey in the dark" means that, in the long run, physical appearances are not important.

Cheese: Sacred to the Greek god, Apollo, it represents things coming to fruition. The term "big cheese" refers to a boss, or someone successful and in charge.

Rolled Paper: This represents the written word. It can take the form of a contract, or can be a prize of some kind. It usually signifies that financial gain is about to be the reward for hard labor.

Card Meaning

The Nine of Wands represents defending what is yours from others. You have worked long and hard to achieve a specific goal and the end is in sight. All the fire and creativity of the Wand suit is about to pay off, and it is time to focus your energy for one final push towards the finish line. The issue is, now that you have something real and tangible, you have also become most acutely aware of the possibility of losing it. You feel that others are trying to prevent your success, and want to take the prize away from you.

This is the time to step forward and defend what is yours, as you deserve to be rewarded for your efforts. This card implies a justifiable form of aggression, but as always, there are two sides to everything. It is important to know the difference between truth and paranoia. Now is the time to examine your motives and to be aware of the dangers and pitfalls of the ego.

Take a lesson from the cats and realize that appearances are often deceptive. The man holding the cheese so tightly to him is in danger of crushing it and, therefore, losing it altogether. He is going nowhere and wasting energy on trivial distractions.

The shadow aspect of this card is that you are unable to relax your vigilance and, therefore, are never able to move forward and forge past insults or injuries.

Kitchen Wisdom

Focus your attention. Don't trip over the cat because you are looking over your shoulder for a tiger.

Ten of Wands

A figure is struggling with two large grocery bags that seem heavy and unwieldy. They occupy the arms and obscure the face, and the clothing is so androgynous that it is unclear as to whether this person is male or female. Let us call her "she." She is attempting to wedge open the door to her house by using her feet, as she is afraid that she will drop the bags if she frees her hand to pull on the doorknob. It does not seem to occur to her that she could simply put the bags down and open the door. There is a monkey on her back that seems to be causing all this confusion. It is reaching around her and grabbing carrots from the bag. One has even fallen onto the ground. There seems to be nothing but carrots in the bags, all to feed that one monkey. One hopes that she will soon be inside the door and relieved of her burdens.

Key Elements

Carrots: In this card, carrots are seen as motivations, as in the old "carrot and stick" metaphor. This system was supposedly first used by the owners of donkeys as a way of keeping the animal moving. A carrot was suspended from a stick and dangled just out of reach in front of the donkey. The theory was that the animal would move forward in order to get the elusive treat, and if it did not, it would get beaten with a stick. As a system, it combines a promised reward with a potential threat. In this card, there are no sticks; both motivation and punishment have been self-induced.

Monkey: The phrase "monkey on your back" describes anything that you find to be a constant burden. It is difficult to reach something on your back, so therefore it implies that your troubles will be hard to get rid of. In recent years, the term has been used in relation to drug habits, but in this card, it signifies anything that is going to keep bothering you or causing you worry.

Card Meaning:

The Ten of Wands is not what you would expect to see as the final card in a cycle of achievement. One would think that there would be more of a celebratory feeling instead of this emphasis on burdens and despair. This card corresponds with the tenth card of the Major Arcana, which is The Wheel of Fortune. In that card, the Wheel is always turning and fortunes are constantly shifting. In this card, the fortune has been achieved, but it has become a heavy burden. The worry is that you can always lose what you have worked so hard to achieve, and the maintenance then becomes the work.

The number 10 symbolizes the completion of a cycle and the moving forward towards another one. It carries the element of progression that is not seen in the number 9, which speaks to the victory itself. The meaning of the Ten of Wands is that your previous accomplishments have turned into burdens, and it is time to put them down and move on to something else.

When you draw this card in a reading, you are being asked to consider what it is that makes you feel weighed down by the burden of responsibility. Is it necessary to shoulder it alone, and are you creating more problems for yourself than you need to be? This card suggests that the solution to these problems is close to hand. It's as simple as putting down the bags and opening the door.

The shadow side to this card is that you like the monkey being there.

Kitchen Wisdom

If you have a monkey on your back, stop buying it carrots.

Page of Wands

A young man wearing a red feather in his headband is busily stirring a pot with a stick that he has cut from a nearby tree. He has made a campfire, and is impatiently trying to bring the water to a boil by further agitating it. The water is spilling over the sides of the pot, and the fire is in danger of being extinguished. A piece of wool from the Page's cloak has become entangled in the stick. Although he has noticed it, he has not removed the thread as it is creating an interesting pattern and he thinks he could be inventing some new form of cooking implement.

Key Elements

Page of Wands

Page: All pages are traditionally considered to be messengers of some kind. They do not necessarily have to be real people, or young people, but they bring to a reading the spirit and attitude of their particular suit. Pages belong to the element earth, as this is where seeds are planted and, symbolically, new ideas begin. The Page of Wands is Earth in the suit of Fire. Fire burns the earth and the earth is made more fertile by the resultant debris. This combination of elements gives the Page his passion and energy, which serves as the perfect catalyst for new ideas and inventions.

Stick or Branch: This represents the suit of Wands, generally thought of as the first suit of the Minor Arcana, if one were to think of a project as having four stages. Wands are the preliminary start to a venture that begins with an idea or conception. Wands also signify the element of fire that speaks to passion, creativity, and enthusiasm. In this card, a physical wand is being used as a tool to stir things up.

Card Meaning

The Page of Wands is a very busy soul, always trying out new inventions that test the limits of his imagination. He is impatient with things that seem to take too long to work and, as a result, is always darting from one project to another. He has a million different ideas, some of which are brilliant and deserve careful attention in order to bring them to fruition. His earth energy helps to stabilize the creative impulses that the fire side of him wants to let burn out of control.

When you draw this card in a reading, it is time to stir things up a bit. The Page is asking you to look at things from a new perspective—to try something different and to let your imagination run free. It is a call to rouse yourself from inactivity and to participate in this thing called life.

The shadow side of this card lies in the Page's restless nature. There is a tendency to be careless, and this is how mistakes happen. In order to be successful, the Page must balance enthusiasm with practicality. Having said that, being afraid of making mistakes should not prevent trying something new; "nothing ventured, nothing gained" holds true in this card.

Kitchen Wisdom

When you think outside the box,
make sure you have a place to store your ideas.

Knight of Wands

This fellow is the life of the party. He has put a hobby horse head on top of a broomstick and is riding it around, entertaining even as he works, sweeping up the debris. His clothes are brightly decorated and he is blowing a trumpet, although it looks equally as if he could be drinking from a bottle. There is a fireplace smoking in the background, and the Knight is directing all the trash towards its glowing coals.

Key Elements

Knight: A member of the warrior class that represents action and courage. They are the traditional *defenders of the realm*. Knights are identified as possessing the extreme qualities of their individual suits. They are associated with movement, either physical or intuitive, and are therefore seen as catalysts for change. This Knight represents the suit of Wands which is about creative initiative and the passion it takes to start new endeavors. He is charismatic, energetic, and always on the go.

Horse: A symbol of strength, victory, mobility, and freedom. The color of the horse represents the nature of the knight. This horse is purely fictitious. It represents this knight's ability to create an effect by using his imagination and charm. The hobby horse is also a child's toy, a somewhat telling statement regarding this knight's state of maturity.

Card Meaning

The Knight of Wands is about seizing the moment without thought or hesitation. All Knights belong to the element of fire. They are the action figures, or *firebrands*, of the Tarot Court. The suit of Wands is also associated with the fire element. This Knight is fire of fire. He is red hot and blazing a trail that makes it difficult for others to keep up with him. This card is one that speaks of action and implies a fast change or transition.

When you draw this card in a reading, you are being asked to consider the direction that this Knight is moving towards. He faces all challenges with a fearless bravado. To him, life is a party and he is always at the center of it—loud, colorful, and confident. You are being asked to seize the moment before it is lost. You might need to borrow a bit of swagger and elan in order to face a particular project or situation.

The shadow side of this card is that fire can burn out of control as well as heat. The energy of this knight needs to be channeled towards constructive purposes and realistic goals.

Kitchen Wisdom

A one-knight stand leaves you with the dirty dishes.

Queen of Wands

A glamorous woman is applying bright red lipstick with one hand and directing the caterer with the other. This is the Queen of Wands, a regal blend of sexuality and efficiency. She sizzles in her red dress. The long strand of pearls roped around her neck adds to her air of sophistication and drama. A golden crown is sitting on the countertop along with a gaily be-ribboned wooden spoon that looks incongruous amidst the display of wealth. A black cat is standing beside her, looking up and assessing the scene with an attitude that is both watchful and curious.

Key Elements

Lipstick: Red lipstick is associated with passion, sexuality, sophistication, drama, and charisma. It has been reported, that one feels more *capable* when wearing red lipstick, as it is considered an important aspect of *power dressing*. To dream of putting on lipstick represents an aspect of one's personality that feels superior, or more deserving, than others. There is an element of wanting to out-do or out-perform the competition.

Pearls: As one of the oldest gemstones, the history of the pearl is rich with magic and folklore. Early cultures believed that a single drop of rain fell from the heavens and became the heart of an oyster. Pearls are known as *teardrops of the moon* as they are strongly associated with female, water, and lunar cycles. Pearls strung on a thread represent order, and a pearl necklace is said to symbolize cosmic unity. The threads of the necklaces are said to connect spiritual relationships between separate individuals or scattered elements, as each pearl is considered unique. The neck is astrologically associated with sexuality, which adds a physical element to the iconography.

Black Cat: A black cat is traditionally associated with the Queen of Wands. They are mysterious creatures that live by their own set of rules. This innate sense of authority and superiority seems to blend well with the Queen's intelligence and sense of entitlement. They add an air of magic, and speak to those things that will always remain enigmas. They know many secrets and keep them well.

CARD MEANING

The Queen of Wands, like all the Tarot queens, is associated with the element of water. The suit of Wands is associated with the element of fire; therefore, she is water of fire. She is a mixture of emotional maturity, blended with passion and creativity. Imagine a kettle coming to a boil, the steam whistling out, practically vibrating on the stove. This is the Queen of Wands—hot, loud, passionate, the center of attention, and the ultimate project manager.

When you draw this card in a reading, you will need to consider both the energy of the Queen and her cat. You will be required to take charge of a project and somehow stay in the spotlight while exuding an air of quiet authority. It will take a great deal of confidence and an understanding of human emotions to carry this off, as both skill and an undeniable sense of style will be needed.

The shadow side of this card occurs when the water element takes over and douses the flame. It could bring quick temper and quick tears. The wooden spoon pictured in this card is a reminder not to let your ego become over-inflated, as superiority is only effective if it is tempered with humility.

KITCHEN WISDOM

When you have a difficult task ahead of you, put on your red lipstick and walk out the door.

King of Wands

The King of Wands is advancing with outstretched arms as if unable to contain his excitement and enthusiasm. He is holding a contract, eager to show it to the chef who is bowing deferentially as he welcomes him to the restaurant. The red carpet has been rolled out in honor of the king, and it is stamped with the same design of a lion that he wears on his cloak. The chef has many reasons to pay tribute to this king.

Months ago, the king was very impressed by one of the meals he was served, and he asked to meet the cook. The man told the king of his dream of one day owning his own restaurant. Well, that was a project the king could embrace. He called in all his numerous contacts and simply made it happen.

Now the chef is inviting the king to the grand opening and has more than likely made a special dish in his honor.

Key Elements

King: All of the kings represent the power and success of their particular suit. They are also associated with the element air, which allows them intellectual prowess and the ability to make decisions in a fair and rational manner. Wands is a fire-based suit, and the heat is synonymous with passion, energy, and creativity. The King of Wands is air of fire. It is a potent combination as oxygen fuels fire, making it burn even brighter. He is a natural leader as his charismatic personality draws people to him, like moths to a flame. Like those ill-fated moths, a few unfortunate souls have been singed by his quick temper and impulsive gestures that happen when his fire burns out of control.

Lion: The lion has been termed "King of the Jungle," or "Lord of the Land," and is often compared to the eagle, which reigns supreme in the air. The lion symbolizes courage, strength, bravery, fearlessness, and royalty. Lions are also associated with protection of the family, as the males do not commonly hunt, but instead, they watch over and protect their prides from threat. In Heraldry, which is the study of Coats of Arms, the position of a lion is significant. A lion seen in profile, walking with its right paw raised is called a *lion passant*. It signifies protection rather than aggression.

Staff with Leaves: This staff, or branch, is particular to the suit of Wands, and symbolizes the life force that is present in all acts of passion and creativity. The leaves are growing out of a branch that is not connected to a tree, or even planted in the ground. The force of one's will is enough to make the sap flow as the bud of an idea becomes a fully formed leaf, or concept. There is also a somewhat phallic association to this symbol.

Card Meaning

The King of Wands is about being an entrepreneur. He is considered to be a goal-oriented and highly motivated facilitator of all projects that require a vision in order to make them succeed. He is not necessarily the one to come up with the original idea, but he knows how to get people to work together, and the power of his personality allows others to trust him, even as he takes large risks.

When you draw this card in a reading, the robust energy of this king is about to enter your life. You will either need to borrow this energy in order to perform a leadership role, or you will be visited by someone possessing such characteristics. Virility is always an asset in the bedroom or the boardroom.

This is a powerful card to have when you need to take control of a situation. As with all the fire signs, energy is best used when it is clearly directed towards a certain purpose. Fortunes can be made and lost in the blink of an eye, so you need to exercise a little caution and monitor impulsive tendencies. Remember the moths.

The shadow side to this King is that he is prone to a quick temper, and can be ruthless and manipulative in getting what he wants.

Kitchen Wisdom

When you need to coordinate a major event, choose your team wisely and delegate well—especially for the clean-up process.

Ace of Cups

The steam from a pot of tea is drifting in and out of the cup into which it has been poured. The shape of a heart is formed as it wafts away and curls into a traditional poster of The Ace of Cups that is pinned to a wall. The steam then drifts towards the painting and seems to mingle with the five streams of water that are shown flowing out of a golden goblet. A bird is holding a ribbon in its mouth. As the ribbon falls, it becomes water flowing into the cup.

The face of the woman who is pouring the tea is invisible to us, but, we sense that there is a smile on it as she lifts the rounded white pot. There is a cheerful design of bright red hearts on her tea set. The cup itself rests on a round table, covered with a cloth that is alive with the pattern of lotus blossoms. It is a warm and welcoming scene, and we can almost hear her say, "Shall I be Mother?"

Ace of Cups

Key Elements

Tea: Tea cultures vary across the world. In Japan, there are numerous tea ceremonies that symbolize anything from good luck in a marriage to an apology for a wrong doing. In Baltic culture, one is considered to become part of the family after sharing a third cup of tea. To set aside time for tea means to set aside one's personal concerns and to focus on building a relationship with others. In Britain, a cup of tea is the cure for anything from a headache to a near-death experience. To dream of a teapot indicates that one is having concerns regarding the heart, emotions, or the circulatory system. The teapot itself can be considered the wellspring of warmth and unconditional love.

Lotus: The lotus grows in shallow, muddy water. These are generally considered unfavorable conditions, yet the blossoms are magnificent and never seem to have a drop of mud on their petals. Due to this ability to thrive under adverse circumstances, they have become symbols of motivation. They are highly prized in Hindu and Buddhist religions as symbols of youth, beauty, life, and spiritual grace. In this card, they symbolize a blossoming of consciousness, or emotional awareness.

Card Meaning

All Aces are symbols of new beginnings. They are the power players of the Tarot deck, and, in a reading, these trump cards can upstage even the Major Arcana. As the first cards in a suit, Aces set the tone for all the others that follow after them.

The Ace of Cups is the source of emotional wellbeing, brought about by unconditional love. This kind of warmth is most often associated with the maternal archetype. The teapot, as a vessel, represents the source of all such emotions. The act of pouring liquid from a central source to smaller, waiting vessels is synonymous with receiving little blessings, a social form of Communion. In traditional cards, five rivers are seen to flow from one central cup, to represent the awakening of the five senses.

When you draw this card in a reading, it means that you are on the cusp of a new emotional awakening. It could involve a relationship with another person, either another adult, or a parent, or a child, or it could progress along more spiritual or philosophical lines. It is a very positive card, and how this proceeds will depend on how willing you are to open your heart to fresh experiences.

A cup is not always full and often not overflowing, but with this card, you can feel the warmth that is being extended to you.

The shadow side of this card is that tea can grow cold if it is not consumed. It is always a risk to open your heart, but the consequences of not doing so are equally disastrous.

Kitchen Wisdom

An offer of a cup of tea is a kindness, and that is a good beginning.

Two of Cups

Two lovers, wearing similar bathrobes, are holding hands while standing in front of the breakfast table. Two cups of coffee bearing caduceus symbols are waiting for them, as is a bowl containing a whisk and two eggs. In the background, a rug with a primitive lion pattern lies in front of a neatly made bed. They have not noticed that the price tag is still attached. A double heart is traced over the entire scene, tying all the elements together.

Key Elements

Clasped Hands: Two hands joined together symbolize a partnership or allegiance. In the business sense, this is shown as a handshake, and a great deal of emphasis is placed on the firmness of the grip indicating the solidity of the intentions. In this card, the hands are grasped one on top of the other to show that both passive and active principles exist in a relationship.

Caduceus Symbol: The Caduceus of Hermes—two snakes intertwined on a rod, facing each other at the top—has been mistakenly associated with the medical profession. This came about due to an error in the interpretation. The Rod of Asdepius, designed with a single snake or serpent, is the symbol that is associated with the son of Apollo, who was skilled in medicine, and it is used as a symbol of healing and regeneration. The caduceus stands for negotiation, commerce, eloquence, and even trickery. The two serpents represent duality: the light and the dark, or the ability to see both sides of an issue. In this card, it represents the balancing of opposing forces that needs to occur in order to maintain a stable union.

Lion: The Lion is king of the jungle. He symbolizes not only strength and passion, but the inherent carnal nature of man.

CARD MEANING

In Numerology, 2 represents duality. The number two can be divided into individual sections and this can mean love and kindness as well as the ability to corrupt. One can look at the shape of a heart and see either a joining of two question marks or a joining of two twos. The double heart shown in this card addresses the ideal situation, and shows that harmony can be created by the bringing together of opposites.

The Two of Cups is about the starting of a new partnership, whether romantically or otherwise. It does not have the same intensity as the Lover's card in the Major Arcana because it has not yet been tested by time. In this card, the price tag still remains on the rug. The decision has been made to join forces, but the outcome has not yet been determined.

When you draw this card in a reading, it is usually a very positive sign. The anticipation and excitement of a new relationship brings with it all the power that is created by strong emotional connections.

The shadow side to this card lies in the other aspects of the number two, which are to be two-timing, two-faced, or to speak with a forked tongue. It is a warning against duplicity of any kind. The key to harmony lies in balance, and you are being asked to use whatever differences that you find to complement rather than hinder progress.

KITCHEN WISDOM

It takes two to tango, and two to tangle. Learn how to dance.

Three of Cups

Three generations of women are seated around a circular table, at the center of which sits a large teapot. They are all participating in the ritual of giving and receiving. Each woman is holding a cup of tea in her right hand, offering it to her neighbor. Her left hand is open to accept a cup for herself. It is a sunny day, and the steam from the cups mingles in the air. A bird perches on a nearby fountain, as if waiting for the steam to produce drops of water for it to either drink or bath in. There is an atmosphere of carefree celebration with not a cloud in the sky.

Three of Cups

Key Elements

Three Generations of Women: The symbolism of the Triple Goddess is generally spoken of in reference to the three phases of the moon: waxing, full, and waning. These represent the three phases of a woman's life: maiden, mother, and crone. For the purpose of this card, the three generations demonstrate the life cycle by connecting the feminine qualities of each era. Youth corresponds with new beginnings, excitement, and anticipation; the mother is at the peak of her power and describes fertility and stability; while the grandmother represents wisdom and compassion. These qualities, although considered female, are not restricted to the female sex, hence the phrase, "Get in touch with your feminine side."

Teapot: With tongue in cheek, the strength of the entire British Empire could be said to rest on the humble teapot. It is also seen at the center of Asian ceremonial culture. Our little teapot invokes a world of tradition and meaning: home, comfort, and contentment in one hand, and respect, honor, and obedience in the other. The suit of Cups is linked to the element of water, and together represent our emotional response to the world. As water is the very essence of life, a teapot could be seen as the crucible that contains our emotional stability.

Bird: Birds are connected with the element air and represent both a lightness and a spirituality. They demonstrate a higher level of thought.

Card Meaning

The Three of Cups is about breaking away from the intimate circle of two, and allowing others to be part of our emotional framework. It is about celebrating our good fortune by socializing with others. It is also a card of networking and communication. This is a gentle card and, if career success is to be furthered, it cannot be obtained through typically masculine "power meetings," but rather through more relaxed and convivial gatherings. This card is also seen as two separate forces joining to form a third, so either childbirth or a new partnership are implied.

The shadow side of this card could mean that too much time has been spent socializing, and it is time to start paying attention to more practical and less hedonistic pursuits.

Kitchen Wisdom

It's often not what you know, but who you know that matters.

Four of Cups

A baker, still wearing his apron, sits with folded arms and downcast eyes. In front of him is a table covered by a cloth, beautifully patterned with vines and leaves. On this cloth sit three empty measuring cups forming a casual triangle. Beside him, on his right side, a large dog sits patiently holding its dinner bowl in its mouth. Also on the right side, but behind him, the baker is being offered a glass of champagne that sends bubbles into the air around him.

He remains oblivious to all this activity, ignoring both his responsibilities and the pleasures that are being offered to him. Is he asleep, or is he truly disinterested?

Key Elements

Measuring Cups: The number 4 is a symbol of measurement. There are four points of direction—four seasons, four limbs of man, and four chambers of the heart, to name a few examples. The fourth dimension corresponds to time, or rather the illusion of it. Four is the first solid number and represents wholeness and a sense of order in the Earth. The three measuring cups speak to this notion of rational assessment and calculated appraisal, yet there is an uneven number of them, which defies the entire concept of the ordered square. The cup that is being offered is flute-like and frivolous by comparison, yet it completes the solidity of the number four. The message in this card is that not everything can be subjected to the same analysis; some qualities and emotions are more ephemeral and remain immeasurable.

Dog: Historically, dogs have remained man's best friend: a domesticated animal that is the symbol of unconditional love and loyalty. In order to deserve such a blessing, there are responsibilities, such as feeding, housing, and exercising that must be carried out in order to create a harmonious relationship. The gift of love and the responsibility of ownership are inseparable. The baker is not paying attention to his dog, as he is so certain of his loyalty. This card is describing the cost of being oblivious, as the man is not even aware that he is being forgiven.

Card Meaning

The Four of Cups is about being dissatisfied with your current emotional situation. The glow of the couple as seen in the Two and the fun found in networking as seen in the Three has worn off. When taking measure of your life, you notice that the cups are empty. You feel bored and somewhat depressed. Cups by nature can only hold stagnant fluid. It takes the action of pouring, mixing, and blending to create motion or flow. If you sit and stare at three empty cups, you will indeed feel like something is missing from life in general.

When you draw this card in a reading, you are being asked to consider those things that you might be taking for granted. If you look around and count your metaphorical blessings, and continue to feel that your life is empty, then it is time to do something about it. The Four of Cups wants the return of stability.

It might be that you are simply unaware of what is being offered. You have been too self-absorbed to look around and pay attention. The other possibility is that you have been offered all the wrong things and they no longer hold interest for you. Only you can know if your current lifestyle is working in a positive and healthy way. Whatever the case may be, it is time to get up and feed the dog!

The shadow side to this card lies in self-absorption and the inability to see beyond the narrow confines of ego.

Kitchen Wisdom

Anonymous prayer seen on a bumper sticker,
"Dear God, help me to be as good a person as my dog thinks I am."

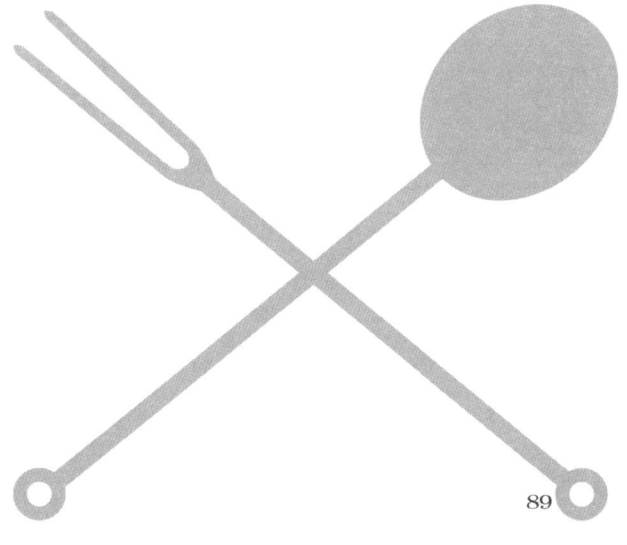

Five of Cups

A forlorn-looking woman wrapped in a bathrobe sits on the kitchen floor. On the counter is a jug of milk and, beside it, three glasses are in the midst of spilling their contents onto the floor. Moonlight sets the scene, shining through an open window. Two glasses are set on the windowsill in the proverbial half-empty, half-full fashion. They shine brightly in the dark, as does the water that is pouring out of an open faucet. The only creature that looks even remotely hopeful in this desolate situation is the cat that is getting ready to lap up huge quantities of milk. He cannot believe his good fortune.

Five of Cups

Key Elements

Five Glasses: Glasses, or cups, hold water—synonyms for holding emotions. The spilled contents refer to tears. The three cups on their sides point to sorrow and loss, and they speak of an empty or broken heart. The two cups that remain upright on the windowsill provide an option. They could symbolize hope, or give reason for even further pain, depending on how the level of their contents is viewed.

Running Water: Water, as we know, is a symbol for emotions. This water is running unchecked and unheeded from an open tap. There is a sense of waste and futility, as such grief seems out of all proportion to the situation. We ask ourselves: "Why doesn't she just turn the tap off?"

Moonlight: La Luna, leading to the word *lunatic,* conjures thoughts of wild and crazy nights and a loss of innocence. Moonlight is also reflected light and therefore aptly corresponds to reflecting our thoughts and feelings. It may also serve to deepen our confusion and inner conflict.

Card Meaning

This is the crying-over-spilled-milk card taken to its most literal level. There have been definite events in life that have caused either minor disappointments or major heartache and grief. This is a card that confirms that things are not going well. The events have been beyond our control and all that is left to do is clean up the debris. In the middle of the night, the sense of isolation is even more intensified. When these events occur, we all have to go through a period of mourning. This card is addressing the somewhat exaggerated response to an event, because we cannot see any positive outcome. The milk has been spilled, but because we have our heads down, we cannot see that the cat is happy.

It is not a constructive response to a bad situation to curl up in a bathrobe thinking, "Oh poor, pitiful me." When you draw this card in a reading, it means that you need to find the bright side of things. There are still two upright glasses well within reach.

The caution, or shadow, that lies in the half-filled glasses is that our expectations could be unreasonable. Healing usually takes place with tiny steps, not giant leaps.

Kitchen Wisdom

Don't cry over spilled milk. You might have been lactose intolerant, anyhow.

Six of Cups

A young boy and girl sit outside on a colorful rug. They are having a tea party with their friends, and included in the festivities are such celebrities as the Velveteen Rabbit and Winnie the Pooh. They are acting out traditional adult roles by playing house. It is amusing that the girl is pouring the tea for a boy who has a slightly bewildered expression on his face. The animals, however, are all very clear as to what is expected of them, and seem to be enjoying themselves immensely. The sun is brightly shining and the garden is safely protected by a large hedge that circles it. Houses can be seen in the background, meaning that the children are not too far from home.

Key Elements

Tea Party: A time-honored childhood tradition. It is how adult roles are interpreted and fantasies are acted out. We learn the art of hospitality, as well as the benefits of both giving and receiving. This get-together symbolizes friendship, trust, innocence, and security. There is no implied danger, rather it is a moment, caught in time, of enjoying life's simple pleasures. If it were an adult gathering, tea leaves could be read. It is doubtful that our young friends are skilled in this regard; however, there is an aspect of "what the future holds" in this scene that serves to further emphasize that fleeting period of innocence called childhood.

Card Meaning

The Six of Cups is a card that some relate to whimsy and nostalgia, but is really about revisiting those lessons learned in childhood in order to bring some kind of emotional balance to a chaotic adult lifestyle. Not everyone has had an idyllic past, but the lessons to be found in children's literature remain universally true. Margery Williams, author of *The Velveteen Rabbit*, put it very eloquently by saying, "Real isn't how you are made. It's a thing that happens to you. Sometimes it hurts." And of course, there is the wisdom of Pooh: "Poetry and Hums aren't things which you get, they're things which get you. And all you can do is go where they can find you."

When you draw this card in a reading, you are being asked to reconnect with your past. It may be as simple as seeking "out a friend and relation," or it may involve more esoteric skills, such as forgiveness and trust. This is a card that implies a gentle happiness and a seeking out of friendship, after all, "It is hard to be brave, when you are a very small animal."

The shadow side of the Six of Cups lies in clinging to childhood and refusing to move forward. If you are stuck in the past, now is the time to give it up. Old grudges, romances, and dogmas can be safely stored in the toy box where they belong.

Kitchen Wisdom

Once again to quote the great Winnie the Pooh: "Don't underestimate the value of doing nothing, of just going along, listening to all the things you can't hear, and not bothering." Amen.

Seven of Cups

A bridegroom wearing a prayer shawl and yarmulke is balancing on his left leg. His right leg is raised, poised and ready to complete the "breaking of the glass" portion of the ceremony, which symbolizes that imperfection is part of the natural state of things. In a departure from the traditional ceremony, there is a long table stretched out beside him on which lie seven golden goblets. Each one is filled with objects that symbolize a simultaneous blessing and curse.

How the bridegroom views these objects are a clue as to his level of awareness or self-delusion.

Seven of Cups

Key Elements

The Seven Golden Goblets: The concept of the seven goblets loosely corresponds with the seven blessings, or "Shevah Berachot," spoken in the traditional Jewish wedding ceremony. That is where the similarity ends. In more traditional decks, the Seven of Cups are shown resting on a cloud, so as to seem unreal and unattainable. Here, they are solidly planted on a table. The illusions lie completely in how they are viewed.

FIRST GOBLET: Is full of red wine that is spilling onto the floor. This can be seen as an offering, a symbol of respect, a sign of good luck, or it can be translated to mean that blood has been spilled and there is "bad blood" between family members.

SECOND GOBLET: Is full of jewelry, a symbolic treasure trove. This could imply an emotional bounty or it could point towards a selfish desire for material goods.

THIRD GOBLET: Contains a frog. In many cultures, frogs are symbols of good luck and fertility. They also represent transformation to a higher state of awareness. In Western fairy tales, Prince Charming was cursed into becoming a frog, hence the aphorism: "You have to kiss a lot of frogs to find a Prince."

FOURTH GOBLET: Contains a naked woman. Nudity is often a symbol for feeling exposed or vulnerable. The blessing is that the "naked truth" about the betrothed will cause a strong and lasting bond as opposed to one that is held together by artifice.

FIFTH GOBLET: Contains a red car. A car is a physical structure and represents one's "drive" or motivation. To dream of a flying car is to rise above your troubles. It could also symbolize travel or a desire to escape.

SIXTH GOBLET: Contains a woman holding a purse. According to Freud, a purse represents either female genitalia or the womb, maybe because a purse can be either open or closed. This can be seen as a desire for children or a sign that someone else is controlling the purse strings.

SEVENTH GOBLET: The castle could be seen as a symbol of comfort and security, or it could represent ambition and unrealistic goals.

CARD MEANING

The suit of Cups is related to emotions and feelings. As cups can be either empty or full, reactions to a situation can carry either positive or negative overtones. The Seven of Cups, called the *card of illusion*, speaks of what is real and what is not. Self-delusion is synonymous with unrealistic expectations and imaginary hopes and fears. This card at its most extreme addresses issues of mental illness, such as delusions and paranoia. On a more ordinary level, the concerns are those of self-awareness and motivation. At its simplest level, this card indicates that you cannot choose between the many options that are presented to you.

When you draw this card in a reading, it means that there is an element of confusion in your life. You are in a state of wishing and wanting. You are focusing your desires on either a person, an object, or a goal without really understanding the reality of the situation. If your wish was granted, would it become a blessing or a curse?

The shadow side to this card lies in not recognizing the difference between self-delusion and wishful thinking.

KITCHEN WISDOM

To quote Benjamin Franklin:
"If a man could have half his wishes, he would double his troubles."

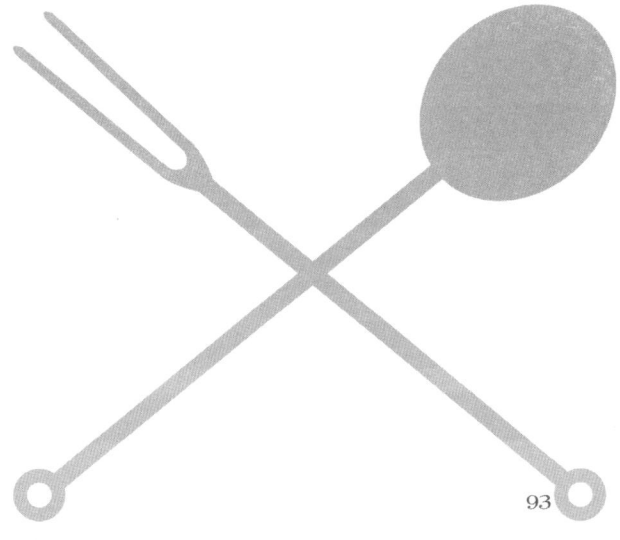

Eight of Cups

Eight of Cups

The evening sun is shining through an open door, illuminating eight drinking vessels. Five of them are lying half-submerged in a basin full of soapy water. The remaining three stand on either side of the basin, not yet emptied. The dishwasher has abandoned his task, escaping barefooted towards the light. The lure of freedom is stronger than his desire to complete the task at hand.

Key Elements

Cups: It would be very easy to create a balance by separating the eight cups into two groups of four. It is significant that, in this card, this is not the case. Cups are vessels that contain fluid and symbolize an emotional state of mind. Five of the cups are tilted on their sides, immersed in water. This implies confusion and suppressed desires. They are also in the process of being cleaned in a way that describes a baptism or transformation. The five cups in the basin represent a recognition of negative or detrimental feelings and a willingness to leave them behind. The three cups that are standing alone represent those areas in life that remain unresolved. The implication is that there is still emotional *baggage* that needs to be dealt with.

Water: The type of water in the scene describes the state of the unconscious mind. In this case, the water in the sink is contained, yet turbulent. The objects are half-submerged, as if there is a strong need to keep one's head above water in order to prevent drowning. There are strong emotional currents that are suppressed or blocked. The small wave that is flowing over the edge of the sink means that there is a way out of this dilemma, a way to move forward. The static water in the upright vessels symbolizes the status quo. Literally, nothing is moving, the glass remains either half-empty or half-full.

Feet: In some cultures feet are considered to be the holiest part of the body, as they represent a very real connection to the world, a means of being *grounded*. Bare feet can symbolize either innocence or poverty. In this card, the feet appear to be relaxed and carefree, as if heading off to a new adventure. In dream symbolism, the sight of an exposed sole means that something you don't fully understand is about to happen.

CARD MEANING

The Eight of Cups represents an emotional imbalance that causes you to walk away from a present situation in order to find what you believe to be missing. There is a dissatisfaction with the way things are and a yearning for a better life. Most often this is a step in the right direction and a necessary part of self-development. It involves recognizing that in order to succeed you have to turn your back on whatever it is that you hold familiar because it is too confining. According to Joseph Campbell, you have to "follow your bliss."

When you draw this card in a reading, you should notice that the person walking away does not have both feet on the ground. There is an element of impracticality to this situation. The question is whether or not this is of any consequence to you. Sometimes you need to just *walk away*, and other times you need to complete certain tasks before making the *big move*. Whatever the case, there is no question that a change in direction is needed.

The shadow side of this card lies in the impulsive nature of discovering a higher calling.

KITCHEN WISDOM

Put one foot in front of the other and keep moving forward.

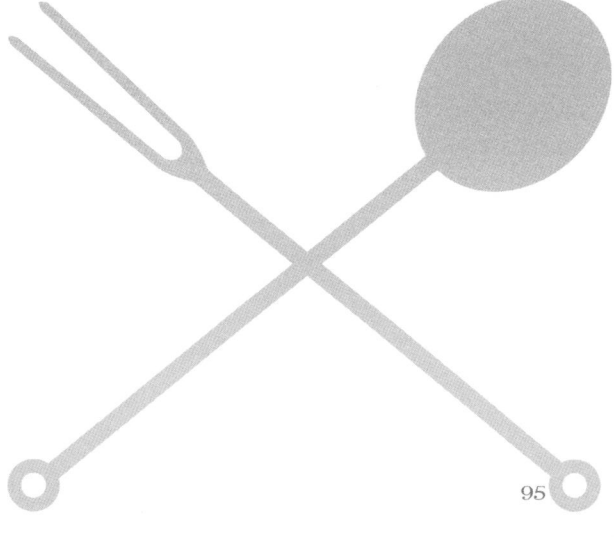

Nine of Cups

Although it is dark and cold outside, it is warm and festive inside. An elderly woman wearing the traditional red hat and purple dress of her society is having a sip of eggnog before her guests arrive. The table is as round and glowing as a full moon, and the cups around the punch bowl are filled to the brim. Her celebration of the holidays has never been more meaningful, as she feels that in her own winter years she has finally come to appreciate the richness of her life. A silent toast is raised, "May all your dreams come true."

Key Elements

Red Hat: The Red Hat Society was officially started in 2000 as a way for women over the age of fifty to enter their middle ages with humor and elan. The Society started with the impulsive purchase of a red fedora in a thrift shop, and has become a worldwide trademark for female bonding and celebration. The beauty of the Society is that it defies the commercial concept that only the young and beautiful can truly enjoy life. Another kind of wide-brimmed red hat is presented to a new cardinal by the Pope. It is a symbol of rank in the Catholic Church. There is no official connection between the two societies.

Punch Bowl and Cups: There are a total of nine cups, all of which are full. Cups are the suit of the Minor Arcana that are associated with the element water, and, therefore, all vessels are seen as symbols for the containment of emotions. These cups are full, meaning that a level of complete satisfaction has been achieved. It is significant that these cups are set out as invitations and for the enjoyment of others. Only one cup has been taken for personal use.

CARD MEANING

The Nine of Cups has traditionally been called the *wish* card or the *wish fulfillment* card, in that you will get whatever it is that brings you emotional satisfaction. In this card, the emphasis is more on recognition. To wish or to want something, implies that you do not as yet have it. The woman in this card has all and more than she needs, and the pleasure is found in sharing her bounty with others.

In numerology, nine represents the end of a cycle. It is the summation of all that you have experienced and learned since you started at zero. Ten then is the *tidying up of loose ends* and the preparation to start all over again. Nine is the moment to bask in the glow of utter contentment.

When you draw this card in a reading, it is important to distinguish which cup is yours. Are you the one holding the full cup, or is it sitting on the table, waiting for you to pick it up? In any case, this is a very positive card. It is an act of consciousness to recognize that there is only a very subtle distinction between the act of giving and the act of taking, if the intention is the same. It is all about harmony and balance as give and take provide an equalizing flow. When you reach the Nine of Cups, the shifts between the two are very small. At this point in time you are complete.

The shadow side to this card involves a lack of recognition, and you think that you need more cups to make you happy. Conversely, there could be an element of smugness if you think all the cups are yours and yours alone.

KITCHEN WISDOM

Cheers!

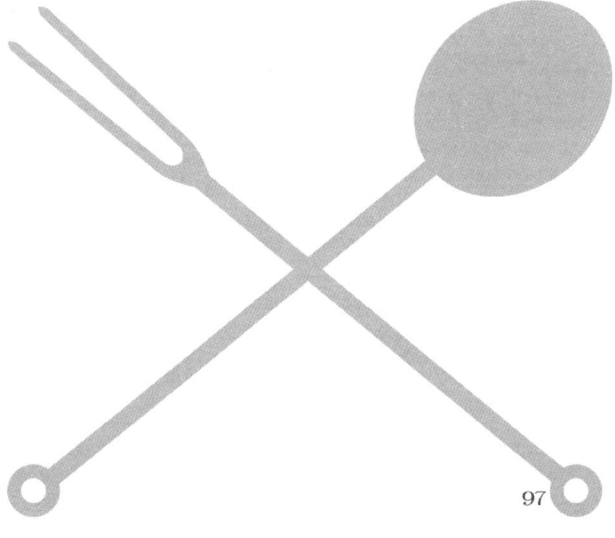

Ten of Cups

At first glance, one sees a happy family gathered around the table. The grandfather carves and the grandmother holds a serving dish, while the young couple gaze happily at the baby in a high-chair. It is a scene of domestic contentment. On closer inspection, the viewer understands that he is outside the family circle and viewing them through a window with four panes of glass that have been nailed shut, as if barring entry. To add an even more surreal quality to this card, a large goblet with a rainbow arching out of it has been superimposed on the window of the house. Even though drops of rain are seen falling outside, the family is warm and contented under their rainbow and the viewer is left wondering if he is hallucinating.

Key Elements

Rainbow: A single ray of light can be broken into seven perceived colors that only become visible when the sun reflects its light through drops of water. This natural phenomena has taken on mystical proportions, arguably since the dawn of mankind. Early Christians saw the rainbow as God's promise to the world that it would never again be destroyed by flooding. Other religions or civilizations have seen the rainbow as a bridge to the heavens, a messenger to the gods, or as the divine Archer's bow. Much has been made of the uniform arch of colors; indeed they have been described as a correspondence to the seven layers of consciousness that lead one from ignorance to enlightenment. The colors also follow the seven chakras, or points of energy, that are located along the body.

>RED: The root, located near the spine, denotes strength, vigor, and outward good.

>ORANGE: The spleen, located in the lower abdomen or womb, denotes creativity, digestive issues, and transcendence to a state of grace.

>YELLOW: The solar plexus, located near the navel, is linked to the mind and represents life force.

>BLUE: The throat speaks to inspiration, communication, and represents truth.

>INDIGO: The mid-brow is the "third eye" or intuition and represents wisdom expressed.

>VIOLET: The crown, located at the top of the head, is about spiritual power and represents ultimate peace.

Card Meaning

The suit of Cups corresponds with the water element and speaks to emotional matters, and how we relate to others on a daily basis. Ten is the number that signifies the end of a cycle or a completion of one set of goals or life circumstances with a need to begin another one. The Ten of Cups is about the ideal family and emotional fulfillment in our daily lives. This card recognizes that not everyone has the same family circumstances, but that there is a visual ideal that has been planted in our heads since birth.

This card is about recognizing that the ideal existence is like the pot of gold under the rainbow. The more you chase it, the further it eludes you. The gold is present in the ten cups, and the recognition that family is the source of emotional fulfillment. It does not have to be the idealized, picture-postcard family; indeed the people you choose to call family do not even have to be related to you. This card is about connecting with others in a way that makes you feel all the colors of the rainbow. It is a very positive thing to get this card in a reading. It signifies an emotional evolution, a moment of blissful recognition that you are complete. Your cups are full, and it has stopped raining.

The shadow side to this card lies in overly romanticizing the ideal to the point where you are unable to be content with your own personal reality.

Kitchen Wisdom

"We must take care of our families wherever we find them."
~Elizabeth Gilbert

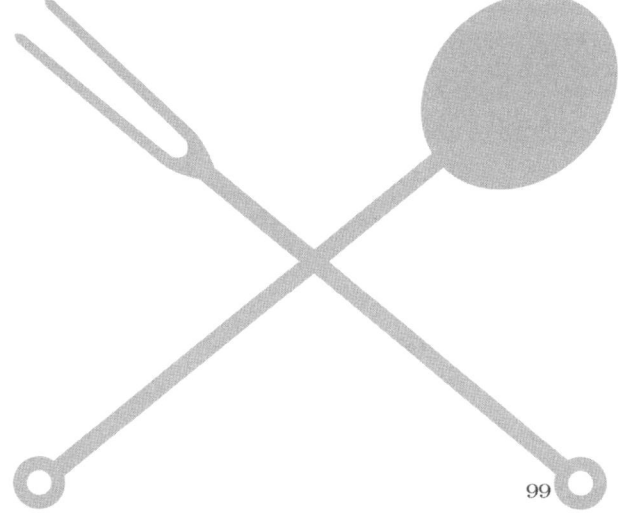

Page of Cups

A young man, with a somewhat effeminate stance and elaborately tied apron, is holding a cupcake in front of him. A single candle has been lit and he looks as if he is getting ready to blow it out and make a wish. The steam from a boiling kettle mingles with the smoke from the candle and they twist and turn together before heading out the open window. A fish is leaping up out of his bowl causing the water to cascade and spill. This card is alive with color and movement. The Page is at the center of the activity, yet does nothing but stare with childlike wonder at the scene.

Key Elements

Page: All pages are traditionally considered to be messengers of some kind. They do not necessarily represent people that you know, or even have to be young people, but they bring to a reading the spirit and attitude of their particular suit. The Page of Cups represents the inner child. He exemplifies those emotions that come with new beginnings. He is sweet and gentle and has a sense of awe while discovering the magic of life.

Goldfish in a Bowl: Cups are associated with the element of water. They represent emotions and feelings. The fishbowl, as a vessel, represents an emotional state. The fish is leaping about, and the water is very active, suggesting a playfulness and a happy anticipation. In this card, the fish represents an element of the unpredictable.

Card Meaning

All pages are associated with the element earth, and conjure images of seeds that have been planted in fertile soil. The Page of Cups is earth in the suit of Water. A perfect combination for growth and fertility. This Page has often been thought to bring messages of pregnancy or adoption. There is a strong association with children when you draw this card. If you are not thinking along those lines, then it is a message to explore those innocent and childlike qualities that have perhaps been long forgotten. It is time to delight in a cupcake instead of counting its calories. It is time to laugh at the squealing sound of an old-fashioned kettle, to take a child to the park, to host a baby shower. The possibilities are endless. One thing that you can be certain of when you draw this card is that you will find your emotional satisfaction in the most unusual of places.

Kitchen Wisdom

Listen to your inner child when it says that it is time to come out and play.

Knight of Cups

A blonde-haired knight leans over a table, gazing into a bowl of water as if captivated by his own reflection. He is dressed in armor, a silk shirt, and a flowing yellow cloak. Beside him, a candle burns, its smoke drifts upwards. An unopened envelope lies tucked beside the bowl. The knight has been momentarily distracted from his task of discovering its contents. It has the look of an invitation, but it could be anything. Pinned to the wall behind him is a poster of a stylized white horse and rider. There is a sense of anticipation to this scene because we know that the knight will eventually open the letter and follow its summons.

Key Elements

Knight: A warrior class that represents action and courage, the traditional *defenders of the realm*. In Tarot terms, Knights represent the extreme qualities of their individual suits. They are associated with movement, whether physical or intuitive, and are therefore seen as catalysts for change. All Knights belong to the element of fire. The armor is both symbolically and literally a mode of protection.

Horse: Every knight needs a horse. The color of the horse that they ride represents the nature of the Knight themselves. A horse is a symbol of strength, victory, nobility, and freedom. They are, literally, the vehicles for action. A white horse represents an innocent heart on a chivalrous quest.

Candle: Illumination, whether literal or spiritual, represents light in the darkness. The individual components of a candle also have their own symbolic meaning. The wax represents flesh or humanity, the wick is seen as the soul, the flame is often the godhead, and the light and heat represent love, divinity, and obedience.

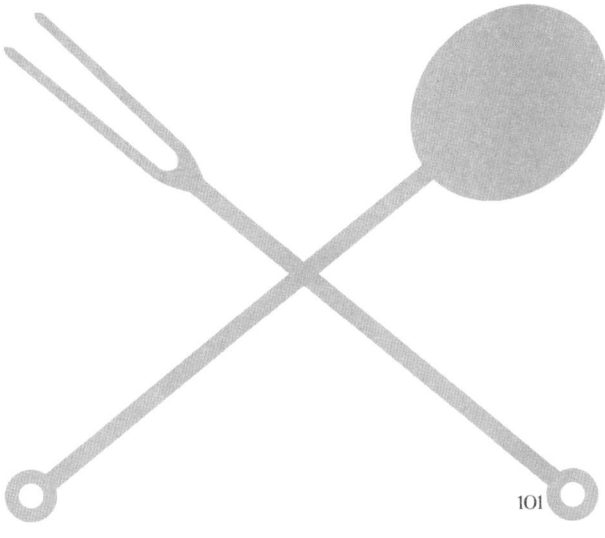

Card Meaning

The Knight of Cups has often been equated with Sir Perceval in his quest for the Holy Grail. There is something romantic, chivalrous, and slightly misguided about this knight. He is the element fire in the suit of Water. His passions are fierce, but quickly doused, as he moves on to the next damsel in distress. There is a spirit of love, beauty, naiveté, and self-absorption in this card. In a reading, Knights urge us to consider the direction that we are moving towards, whether it is to a new romance or some other emotional quest.

It is also time to consider either your own motives, or those of people who you are close to. Do you feel that you need to be rescued? Are you acting helpless and attracting saviors, or are you feeling that others desperately need your help? Innocence and naiveté are often short-lived; so is the bloom of a new romance. This is a card of gazing around before you move forward. The distraction of beauty and charm and the pleasure of a little lightness can be a welcome relief. Just know that the Knight of Cups will be moving on.

The shadow side of this card lies in the extreme nature of this Knight. Either narcissism or an overwhelming savior complex can lead to unhappy endings. Notice that this is the only Knight wearing armor. Self-protection is the key element. Keep it light.

Kitchen Wisdom

A little bit of what you fancy does you good,
but you will be sorry if you eat the whole box of candy.

Queen of Cups

A backdrop of waves crash and fall beyond an outdoor terrace where the Queen of Cups sits on a plush, scallop-shaped barstool. Her hair is piled high and it cascades around her face, as if mimicking the ocean's foam. She is supporting the weight of her head with the palm of her right hand. As she leans against it, her expression is dreamy and distracted, as if listening to faraway voices that only she can hear. The Queen is surrounded by sea shells, and an untouched glass of wine sits beside her. One is hesitant to approach her as she seems so lost in thought, but, in reality, she is waiting for your company.

Key Elements

Queen: All of the Queens in the Tarot Court are associated with the water element. They illustrate the qualities of their individual suits in the way in which they dispense counsel. Queens typically take a more passive role, allowing the kings to act as the aggressors and policy makers. They are, however, the powers behind the throne. Queens are the true diplomats, and tend to get things done with more support and less drama than their counterparts. In a reading, they do not represent a particular female or male person, but rather the spirit of the role.

Sea Shells: The Romans associated shells with the goddess Venus, as she came from the depths of the sea. Shells represent fertility, love, and regeneration. Many cultures also associate shells with prosperity, as they were used as items of currency. A baptismal font is often in the shape of a scalloped shell, representing rebirth and cleansing.

Wine: Wine signifies blood, and blood signifies life. Christian religion associates drinking the blood of Christ with spiritual regeneration. To be drunk on wine is ,symbolically, to become prideful or wise in their own eyes.

CARD MEANING

The Queen of Cups is a water element in the suit of Water—water everywhere. She lives life on a highly emotional level, and all her decisions are based on feelings and intuition. She feels deeply and will understand what you are thinking and feeling even better than you will. The ability for such empathy has given her a reputation for clairvoyance.

She is a supporter of the arts, and has the ability to direct vague feelings or desires into practical courses of action. She will provide all the emotional support that you need in order to believe in yourself and complete a project. This queen is an emblem for maternal or unconditional love, and will nurture all who seek her wisdom.

When you draw this card in a reading, it is time to understand that emotions, like water, need an outlet. If the water is allowed to rise to dangerous levels, dams will burst and flooding will cause serious damage. You are either being asked to assume the role of counselor and comforter, or you are in need of finding one for yourself. This is a good time to listen to what friends are saying and to connect on an emotional level. Guidance is needed.

The shadow side of this queen has to do with all the water in her composition. She can be over-emotional and prone to easy tears. She has also been known to drown her sorrows with an occasional strong beverage.

KITCHEN WISDOM

Comfort food is best served with a side of empathy, and a glass of wine.

King of Cups

The King of Cups is sitting at the head of the table, with his right arm formally raised in toast. He looks calm and in control, but around him things are beginning to fall apart. A large fish tank is seen against the backdrop of a city skyline. The fish are huddling close to the bottom, as some unseen force has caused the water to become agitated and slosh over the sides. In front of the king, a ship-in-a-bottle rocks on waves that have mysteriously appeared. They seem to flood the surface of the table, yet the room remains dry.

The king is splendidly dressed, and a fish amulet holds together the edges of his flowing cloak. Only his left hand, clenched at his side, gives any indication that he is aware of the surrounding chaos.

Key Elements

King: All Kings represent the power and success of their particular suit. The King of Cups controls the watery realms. He represents a person who is closely in touch with the feminine arts of intuition and empathy. As a king, he is associated with the element of air and, therefore, uses his intellectual skills to weigh both fact and emotion before pronouncing a judgment. He is generally an amiable, kind-hearted person, but in times of stress, he can be prone to alcoholic excess and narcissism.

Water: The water in the fish tank symbolizes emotions that have been contained, or controlled. The water that is flooding across the table speaks to those situations that appear out of nowhere, like storm clouds on a sunny day. The king must be cognizant of all the emotional needs of his court and kingdom. The ship-in-a-bottle acts as an emotional barometer. When it starts to be tossed around, the situation is about to go out of control.

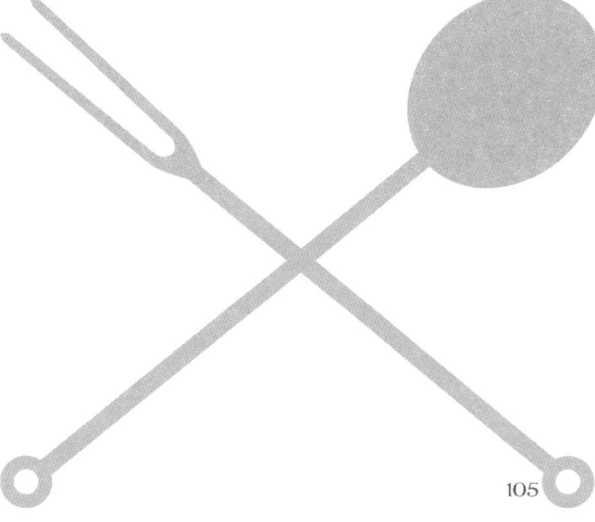

CARD MEANING

The King of Cups is about the battle of the head against the heart. The King has gained an emotional maturity, and he has learned to channel all the romanticism and idealism of his youth into a rational decision-making process. This works very well when the weather is calm and he can display his most charming and generous behavior. This King rules with kindness and compassion and can be a trusted friend and confidant.

When the storm clouds gather and the barometer drops, the King of Cups has to work very hard to maintain control because he is surrounded by the emotional responsibilities of his suit. His natural tendency is to join the drama and drown his sorrows. However, this king tries very hard. He recognizes these tendencies and sometimes over-compensates by becoming too controlling.

When you draw this card in a reading, you are being asked to consider the question of emotional control. Are you being controlled, or are you the one who is calling the shots? Perhaps the weather is fine, and now is the time to exhibit some kingly qualities by being a diplomatic and stabilizing force to those around you.

The shadow side to this card lies in the mood swings that accompany challenging situations.

KITCHEN WISDOM

When you feel the barometer dropping, try to rise above the storm.
Hum "Bridge Over Troubled Waters" until people tell you to stop.

Ace of Swords

A beautifully manicured hand, holding a kitchen knife, emerges from the right side of the card. With one swift motion, the knife slices through the air and two halves of an apple roll across the chopping board. They have been separated with surgical precision to reveal the core of the fruit. The seeds are now visible, exposed and looking for all the world like little nestlings in the womb.

Key Elements

Apple: A fruit rich in symbolism, portraying knowledge, longevity, temptation, and love, as well as discord. The apple has been used for divination because when it is cut in half horizontally, the core forms a pentacle shape. The number of seeds found inside determine the fortune told. In this card, the apple is cut vertically, and the core is now reminiscent of female reproduction, and the seeds look like they are *in utero*. The apple seeds represent the germination or inception of an idea. They symbolize that moment of precognition, before the flash of inspiration occurs that brings a new little bit of brilliance into the world.

Knife: The suit of Swords is associated with the element air, and primarily represents a rational and logical way of processing thoughts and ideas. Like all swords, there is a double-edged quality to their function, and more often than not, lessons are learned the hard way as any sharp edge can cause pain. In this card, the kitchen knife appears from the right side of the card, implying that action will be required in order to bring a concept or goal into fruition. Coming from the left would signify a more passive approach, and denote a period of waiting.

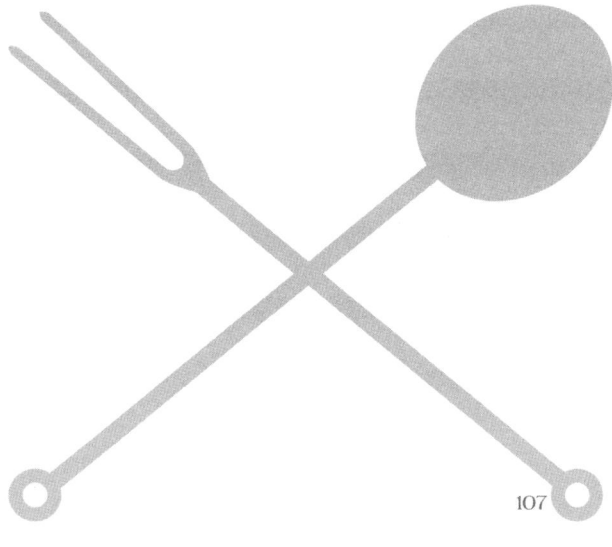

CARD MEANING

The Ace of Swords is the first card in the suit of Swords. Aces set the tone for the rest of their suit. They are the "power players" of a Tarot deck, and in a reading these trump cards can upstage even a member of the Major Arcana.

This Ace leads the way by forcefully exposing the core, or the heart, of the matter. The other cards will then deal with all the issues surrounding dealing with the truth of a situation, and trying to find a balance between logic and compassion, as the head and the heart are often in conflict.

When you draw this card in a reading, it is a signal that you are about to embark on a journey that will lead you towards discovering insight, clarity, and focus. As the hand appears from the right, there will be no easy way to do this. This card is an invitation to discover the truth by cutting through all the protective layers of self-delusion. The challenge will be to reconsider all previous truths and ideals and to decide whether or not they are misconceptions or reality.

The shadow side to this card is that you might not be ready to pull away the layers, and that the core might be too fragile to stand up to scrutiny. If this is the case, go gently, but still go.

KITCHEN WISDOM

When getting ready to hit the nail on the head, make sure your nails look good. Or, stated more simply, if you are heading for a confrontation, look your best. It helps.

Two of Swords

Two knives are embedded in the center of a table. They set the scene for the rest of the card. One knife, or sword, has been used to cut open an apple, and lies in the light, while the other is resting beside a fish, and lies in the shadow. The light and shadow motif travels upward and completely bisects the card. The woman, who is sitting at the table echoes a sense of conflict by placing one of her hands over her heart and the other one over her eyes. The division continues upwards as the architecture separates the action even further. On the light side of the pole, a boat is pointed towards the shore coming home. While on the darker side, a boat is leaving and a small crescent moon appears on the horizon. Both these boats are empty, seeming to be nothing more than the manifestations of an internal struggle between heart and mind.

Key Elements

Hand Positions: The woman's right hand is being used as an effective blindfold. She is covering her eyes as if refusing to look at something that she does not want to see. The blindness is figurative only, as it would take no effort to lift away the hand and open her eyes. Her left hand is placed over the heart, as if in a pledge of allegiance. It is also a protective gesture, shielding that organ from further pain. The positions of both hands are interchangeable and seem to move in opposite directions to the knives on the table, yet they form a poetic symmetry that corresponds to the ripples in the water caused by the movement of the boats.

Knives: The two knives represent the duality that is present in this card. One knife has cut the apple of knowledge, or desire, and lies in the sunlight. The other stands in the shadow beside the fish, a creature of the watery depths representing emotions such as faith and belief.

Boats: Boats travel on the water, and are common metaphors used in describing emotional states of mind. These vessels are both empty and appear to be floating on the tides. They represent the duality that exists within us all. They ride the currents of the mind, seeming in harmony with each other, yet both waiting for the signals needed to change direction.

Card Meaning

If the Ace of Swords sets the stage for uncovering the truth, the Two of Swords begins the journey by describing the absolute sense of duality that is inherent in this notion. The sword's persona is very comfortable when it comes to understanding and dealing with two seemingly opposing concepts of reality. What the heart believes to be true and what the head recognizes as such are often in conflict. The Two of Swords is prepared to accept the dichotomy rather than make a decision.

In general, the number two represents balance and union. It is about making a choice that will further a partnership, define a course of action, or set priorities. The suit of Swords, connected to the element air, is about rational thought and the intellectualizing of emotions. The brain is fighting for dominance over the heart and the struggle is never an easy one.

When you draw this card in a reading, it means that you are attempting to balance two opposing forces. You are either unable or unwilling to make a choice between what you logically know to be true and the emotional consequences of this decision. You can carry on like this for quite a while, but not forever. The Two of Swords accepts that you are not ready to make a choice, but it asks that you recognize that a discrepancy exists. It is the recognition of the situation that is important. The decision at this time is whether to accept it or not.

The shadow side to this card lies in self-delusion, when you will not see that there is a difference between what you know and what you feel. This is when you have to take your hands away from your both your eyes and your heart and see what remains.

Kitchen Wisdom

If you don't like what you see, open your eyes even wider.

Three of Swords

This has to be the worst Valentine's Day ever. A woman is sitting at a table with a look of complete dejection and utter disillusionment. In front of her there is a card inside an open envelope, a bunch of strawberries that are partially chopped, and a container full of fancy cocktail toothpicks. She has taken off her rose-colored glasses and holds half a strawberry in the palm of her hand. It has been stabbed with three of the colored toothpicks that she has taken from the jar. Behind her, a cake topples off its stand, presumably hit by the arrows from Cupid's bow.

Key Elements

Strawberry: A strawberry has a heart-like shape; this is even more evident when it is diagonally sliced into two halves. It is therefore easy to see why they have been associated with love, happiness, and success. In ancient times they were considered symbols of perfect goodness because of the delicious flavor and fragrance. The red color also denotes sensuality, fertility, and abundance. To dream of eating strawberries means that a yearning for love will be fulfilled, or requited.

Three Toothpicks: The number 3 is very significant in the world of numerology. It describes the tripartite nature of the world in such timeless trinities as: Father, Son, and Holy Ghost; mind, body, spirit; past, present, future; and mother, father, child.

Three is the number of communication and interaction. The general idea is that in order to create something new, one must move beyond the confines of the couple or the number 2. The creation of that third entity can be brought about by the union of two to create a unique and separate whole, as in childbirth or other collaborative efforts. Sometimes the creation of that third element comes from separation, as in it takes a third, outside element to break the stalemate and allow movement to occur.

CARD MEANING

The symbol of three swords piercing the heart—the visual metaphor that the woman is holding in the palm of her hand—stands for a separation or parting from a previously held belief and the beginning of a new awareness. The very word "separation" implies pain. A bond has been severed and, because of that, everything has to change. The birthing of a third entity, a unique individual, must now begin.

This card implies a suffering brought about by disillusionment. When you look at the world through rose-colored glasses, everything is artificially tinted to appear, well, rose colored. You take the glasses off and you see the world for what it is.

When you draw this card in a reading, it means that your present reality is causing you pain. It could be that a relationship is going badly, or that you have discovered information that is challenging what you originally believed, whether in love, career, or spiritual matters.

It is ultimately better to know the truth. It is better to be out of an abusive situation than to pretend everything is all right. It is also better to acknowledge the failures and faults of a person or situation and still love them, warts and all. The resultant relationship will be built on acceptance rather than illusion.

The shadow side to this card lies in the inability to move forward. The pain of realization has caused you to come to a standstill. Be patient; pain is the body's way of telling you that something is wrong and you need to pay attention and fix it.

KITCHEN WISDOM

If you have the ability to feel pain, it means you are still alive.

Four of Swords

A young man is lying with his eyes closed in a deck chair beside a swimming pool. He is in a supine, passive position. His arms are by his sides and his belly is exposed. There is a yellow plate with an empty skewer on it, resting on his chest. On a table in the foreground there is a similar plate, except that this one is holding three empty skewers. It is a peaceful scene suggesting rest and regeneration.

Four of Swords

Key Elements

Skewers: Sharp piercing instruments, used most often in the creating of shish-ka-bobs for grilling. In this instance they represent swords. A sword is not only a symbol of strength and authority, but a metaphor that describes the penetrating power of the intellect. The double-edged nature of a sword implies that words can be used to either help or harm a situation. The single skewer on his chest suggests that there is one issue of single most importance that he has to deal with.

Clothing: Traditionally, a knight in full armor illustrates this card. It is of significance that this young man is unprotected, except for cotton shorts. We can rest assured that his genitals will not be burned, but the rest of him is exposed to attack from both the sun's rays and unseen enemies.

Card Meaning

The eyes are considered to be windows to the soul. This young man has his eyes closed. He is not exposing his soul, although he chooses to expose his physical body. He is in a passive, trusting position. He feels safe from attack and is simply enjoying this moment of pleasure. This is not a card of action. It is about recuperation and gaining strength for future action. There is a temporary nature to this card. The skewers are empty, as if all the food has been eaten, and we know that the young man cannot lie in the deck chair forever. The sun will set and he will get cold and hungry again.

When you draw this card in a reading, it means that it is time to retreat. It could imply the need to recover from an illness or an emotional assault. Whatever the cause of previous distress has been, it is now time to regroup and find strength in rest. It is best to take time out from problem solving, as the answers will only come when you leave them alone. You will need all the rest you can get because new struggles lie ahead.

The shadow side to this card lies in a form of passive aggression, refusing to engage in communication, due to either anger or a need to control; this is a form of disengagement that is neither healthy nor restful.

Kitchen Wisdom

A change is as good as a rest.
If you cannot go on vacation, invest in a sun lamp.

Five of Swords

The pageant has come to an end, and the streamers are beginning to rustle and sway as the wind picks up. A beauty queen contestant is laughing gleefully as she carries off not only the cake, but all the serving spatulas as well. She is looking back at two disgruntled finalists who are staring at their empty plates. One of them is holding a crown, and the other is holding her head in her cupped hands. There are many unanswered questions. The woman in the foreground looks as if she is taking the cake away from the others and she is wearing a tiara not a crown. Did she win the cake or is she stealing it? The other women look glum; have they already eaten their share and wish they had more? To understand what is really happening one would have to ask the individuals involved, and even then it would be a matter of deciphering their unique perspectives, as each would have a different story to tell.

Key Elements

Cake: The Bible distinguishes the bread of cakes from common bread, in that the former represents spiritual good and neighborly love, while the latter is signified as love of the Lord, or celestial love. *Dream Dictionary: A-Z Dream Meanings* states that to dream of sweet cake means "… a favorable opportunity for the enterprising." "You can't have your cake and eat it, too," is an English proverb that originated in the 1540s. It means that once you have eaten your cake, it no longer exists, and is used to describe the impossibility of having things both ways. It is also a cautionary tale warning against wanting more than you deserve or can handle.

Five Spatulas: In this card, the spatulas represent swords, as both are sharp and have two sides. The number five represents a time of restlessness that leads to action. This results in change brought about by new life experiences. This type of change is not necessarily smooth or easy to accept. Swords, because they are double-edged, can either help or harm you, and the swords' family seems to learn their life lessons through painful experiences.

Card Meaning

The Five of Swords is about conflict and the perception of winning and losing. There is a phrase regarding "winning the battle, but losing the war" that comes to mind when describing this card. The victory is short-lived and in the end does not bring success. On a superficial level, this card is about taking things that are not rightfully yours. The bad beauty queen has absconded with the cake. It looks to be a simple case of greed or revenge. Judging from the expression on her face, she thinks that she is justified and she is taking great pleasure in her actions. On a deeper level, the victory is a hollow one, for what she is taking is a very trivial thing. A cake will not last very long and really does not mean anything. In the end, it is just a cake and she is wearing the tiara, not the crown.

So, who is the real winner? This is the question that you will need to answer when you draw this card in a reading. Depending on your personal situation, you could be involved in a conflict in which you are either the aggressor or the victim. If you are about to get ahead in a struggle, consider the future consequences before you totally commit yourself to the battle. If you are feeling as if you are being bullied, consider if it might not be more victorious to simply walk away. The bottom line is no one can win every battle; choose the ones that are important and step away from the others.

Kitchen Wisdom

You can't eat your cake and still have it.

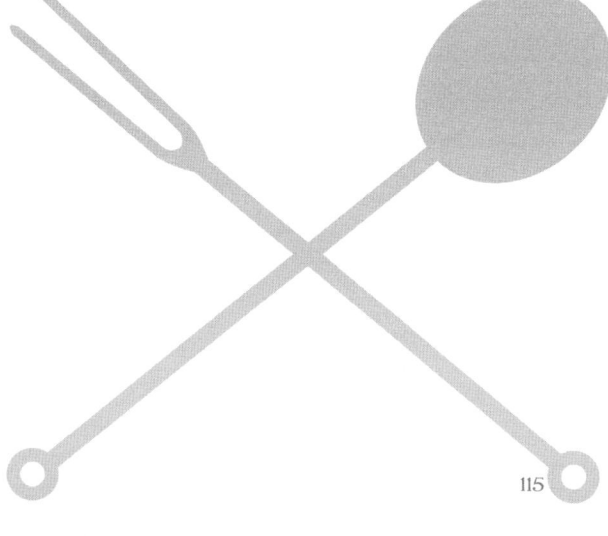

Six of Swords

A woman and her young son are walking out the door. They are both wearing life vests, and appear to be heading towards an empty boat that is moored close by. She is reaching backward with one hand to pull the door closed while guiding the child forward with her other hand.

Sitting on a table in the foreground is a menacing looking set of steak knives in a rack. The shadows of turbulent waves caper and dance around the room, mimicking the pattern on the tablecloth, as if echoing signs of recent upheaval.

Key Elements

Six Knives: They are a representation of six swords. The number six was considered the perfect number by ancient mathematicians. It is also the symbol for Venus, goddess of love, and associated with The Lovers, sixth card of the Major Arcana, and brings with it the same sense of choice and decision making. Six is also considered lucky, as it is the highest number on a dice. The hexagon represents harmony and balance, and it is the shape that bees use when constructing their hives and, therefore, speaks to the values of home, family, and responsibility.

Boat: A boat has many meanings, and the most literal one would imply a trip or a physical journey. Water is synonymous with the realm of emotions and because a boat travels on water it symbolizes an emotional state of mind. If the water is rough, the mind is troubled; if the water is stagnant and unmoving, there are feelings of being trapped and going nowhere. The direction that the boat is pointing in can also symbolize the way one is heading. Coming towards shore could define a homecoming, or a willingness to face a situation. Heading out to sea would indicate a deep desire for escape. This boat is sitting empty, and tied up beside a dock. It is in a state of preparation, or anticipation. The potential is there, waiting to be filled. An empty boat also has a bleak quality to it, as if a deliberate blunting of the emotions has occurred.

Card Meaning

The Six of Swords, in relationship to The Lovers card, implies an emotional decision-making process. While The Lovers speak to new beginnings and commitment, the Swords speak to dissolutions and endings. This card also signifies a journey of some kind; whether it involves physical travel, emotional navigation, or both, depends on your surrounding circumstances.

The woman in this card is walking out of a door. She is leaving a dark interior and moving forward into the bright sunlight. This is a very positive sign in that a period of emotional difficulty or trauma is passing. She is also guiding a child forward. This is a protective or shepherding gesture, and symbolizes a sense of responsibility for the safety and well being of others who depend on you. It also signifies the protection of innocence and child-like purity.

The significance of this card in a reading will depend on how you view the boat. If the scene reminds you of a pleasurable outing, then travel plans are in your future. If you see the boat as a means of escape, you will be making some difficult decisions about leaving your current situation in order to begin a new life.

The shadow side to this card lies in the absence of the ferryman. There will be no guide other than your own strength of commitment. You will need strong life-preserving skills in order to stay afloat, but the effort will be worth it.

Kitchen Wisdom

When you can see the shadows of the waves inside,
it is time to leave. Flooding is imminent.

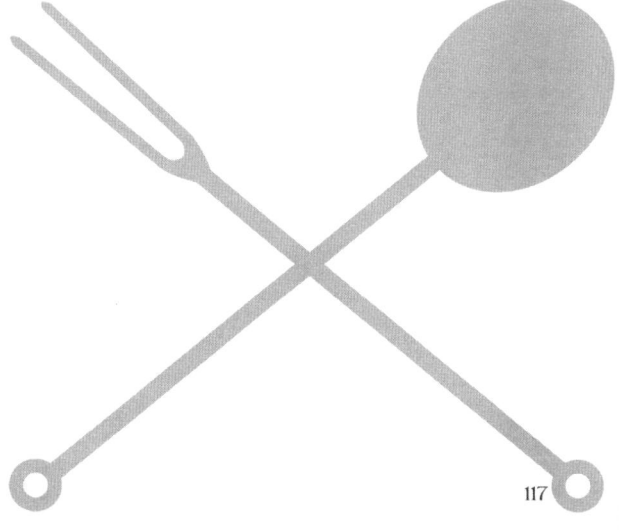

Seven of Swords

A woman dressed in prisoner's stripes is caught in the act of sneaking away from her house. She is tip-toeing towards the yellow taxi that is waiting outside. She has red, high-heeled boots in her hands and a large red bag slung over her shoulder. As she moves forward, a tray of sword-shaped cookies catches her eyes. She hesitates in a moment of indecision. Should she stay or should she go? Should she fill her bag with all the cookies or should she close the kitchen drawer and walk away? Only the cat and dog bear witness to this dilemma.

SEVEN OF SWORDS

Key Elements

Feet: In some cultures, feet are considered to be the holiest part of the body because they are a direct connection to the earth and represent both literally and figuratively a way to remain grounded. Bare feet represent a longing for childhood innocence and freedom. The act of walking on tip-toes implies stealth by wanting to make as little noise as possible. There is also a sense of frivolity and lack of commitment as both feet are not firmly planted on the ground.

Red Boots: Stilletto heels have an erotic connotation, and the color red implies passion. To carry one's shoes shows a personal determination to head in a particular direction. As these boots are so out of keeping with the rest of the outfit, a total change in lifestyle is what this woman is looking for.

Red Purse: According to Freudian symbolism, a purse represents either female genitalia or the womb. One can agree with this, or not, but in any case there is an implied need for either monetary, emotional, or physical fulfillment.

Card Meaning

The Seven of Swords is about being of two minds. The feet are pointing in one direction and the head is looking in another, as if the body and the brain are at odds with each other. It is a card that speaks of impulsive decisions that are perhaps not the most honorable, but very human.

Swords represent the intellect, and a double-edged sword means that your thoughts could either work for or against you. When you draw this card in a reading, you are being asked to consider if your feet are leading you in the right direction.

Often, subterfuge is necessary in order to obtain what you want, and it might work for the immediate period of time. No one lives without a shadow side to their desires. It is part of being three dimensional and life is often quite complicated. This card symbolizes the feeling of being trapped in, or a prisoner of, your own life. It could be a matter of self-deception in that you are not living in a way that is true to your nature. It might be time to change a career, leave a relationship, or fulfill a dream of travelling.

It is time to make a change, but do so in a way that does not cause you regret in the future, if possible.

Kitchen Wisdom

When you call for a taxi, make sure you know where you want to go, and if you can pay for it.

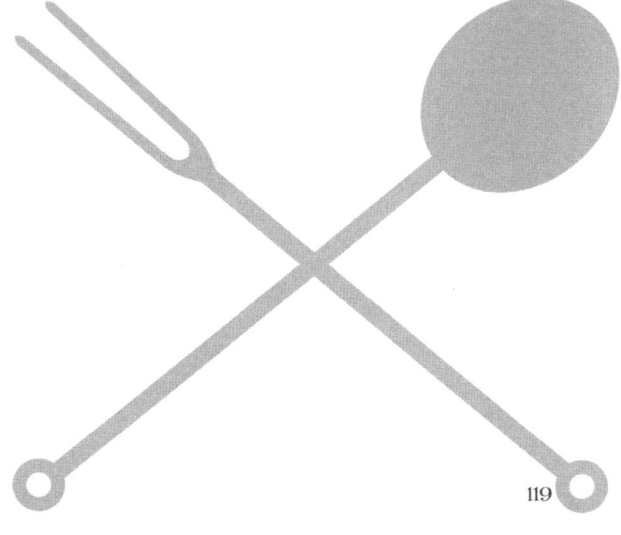

Eight of Swords

A woman in an orange dress and high-heeled shoes is holding a tray of fast-food sliders. They have stylized, sword-shaped toothpicks embedded in them. As she walks by a mirror, she catches sight of herself and sees a very different image. In the mirror she is on her knees, blindfolded, and bound in front of a stove. There is a dead bird beside her. This bird is seen, alive and well in the forefront of the card. It is sitting in a golden cage, even though the door to it is wide open. Through the open window that is behind the woman, there is the slightest hint, or outline, of a bird flying free.

Key Elements

Bondage: The submissive position, blindfold and ropes, all suggest helplessness and immobility. Being on one's knees implies being a victim. A blindfold prevents the ability to see clearly and ropes confine and restrict movement. It is of note that there is no obvious aggressor in the image.

Fast Food: In dream symbolism, eating take-out implies that we are not taking the necessary care of our emotions.

Bird: They are often thought of as disembodied human souls. Birds are free of the constraints of gravity and imply freedom and escape.

Card Meaning

William Blake, in his poem, "London," spoke of "mind forg'd manacles." This is an appropriate description for the Eight of Swords. When you draw this card in a reading, there might be an initial moment of recognition as you identify with the feeling of being stuck with no way out. It does seem hopeless for the bound and trapped woman in the mirror. Ah yes, the mirror! It is important to see that it is not reflecting the reality of the situation, but rather the observer's perception of it.

This card warns against self-imprisonment. As with all of the suit of Swords, it calls for mental clarity. It is time to take a long hard look at the situation and the events that led to this moment. Why do you identify with the victim? What truth are you unwilling to face? What are the obstacles or hurdles that you need to overcome?

This card, despite its initial bleakness, is about taking back power and personal accountability. The cage door is actually open. It has been widely documented that some prisoners have a fear of freedom. The decisions and responsibilities involved with having to care for oneself can be overwhelming, but the only way out is forward. Take it one step at a time.

Kitchen Wisdom

There is no fast-food for the soul.
It's the awareness that will free you, not the shortcuts.

Nine of Swords

Eight skewers sitting in a block of steel dominate the foreground. The diminutive figure of a woman sitting at a table can be seen through the bars. She is holding her head in one hand while the other is limply outstretched, as if reaching for an invisible glass. She appears to be oblivious to the beauty of the brightly patterned cloth that surrounds her. Rising up from her, there is a monstrous shadow that fills the background. It takes the shape of a devil-like being that holds a cleaver in its upraised hand. There is a nightmarish, and very unreal quality to this card.

Nine of Swords

Key Elements

Steel Skewers: These sharp piercing objects are Sword symbols. Swords are related to the element of air and represent the ability for logical thought. They are a means of confronting our fears through discernment and objectivity. Swords are double-edged, so even though they can protect, they can also cause pain. With the family of Swords, most lessons are learned by painful experience.

Evil Shadow: Shadows are caused by the distortion of light as it hits a solid object. This shadow is not reflecting any real presence. It is the product of a fevered imagination. It symbolizes depression, pain, and paranoia that are out of control.

Flower-Patterned Cloth: A symbol of hope. A sign that all is not lost. There is beauty in the world; we just have to be able to open our eyes and see it.

Card Meaning

The Nine of Swords is often called the wake-up-and-worry card. In the dead of night one can feel an overwhelming sense of loss, panic, or fear. Issues of guilt or pain, that are real enough in daylight hours, now take on exaggerated nightmarish dimensions. The good thing is that being a Nine, it means that a cycle is ending. This card calls for action. It is time to confront your demons and slay them with your trusted skewer.

When you draw this card in a reading, it is time to recognize that "there is nothing to fear but fear itself." There are always options, even though they may be difficult and seem impossible. Self-doubt and deprecation is nothing more than a lack of faith in the ultimate benevolence of the universe. It is time to end the situation that is causing you pain and move into the symbolic field of flowers.

Kitchen Wisdom

Everything seems worse in the dark. Turn on a light, and ask for help.

Ten of Swords

A figure in plaid pajama bottoms is dumping a whole roasted chicken into a garbage can. The cook has studded the bird with ten toothpicks as if testing for doneness over and over again. None of the toothpicks have been removed; it's as if each stab has become a reminder of every hurt and insult that has been incurred with the passing of time. The skin is dark brown, even charred, and the term "burnt offering" comes to mind. There is a finality to this scene, and a certain violence, as the ruined dinner has taken on sacrificial overtones. The only light to be seen is coming from the top of the page, as if the sun is just coming up over the horizon. It has been a long night, but dawn is breaking.

Key Elements

Chicken: Chickens were often sacrificed in ancient sunrise rituals in order to ensure a good day as their alchemical properties promoted well being. In Chinese dream symbolism, a chicken is symbolic of pride, because they are the first to greet the dawn and announce their presence to the world. On one hand, they are seen as agents of enlightenment because of their adulation of the dawn. On the other hand, they are seen as symbols for the futility of hope, for darkness always comes.

Garbage Can: The most obvious metaphor is that a garbage can is the receptacle for all the unwanted detritus of life. It is symbolic of getting rid of ideals or previously held beliefs. It signifies the end of a situation.

To dream of a garbage can with an open lid is a reminder that you are safe in releasing the guilt about a particular situation. To dream of throwing something into the garbage means the end of something hurtful, that the healing process is already taking place, and you are able to move into a healthier mental space.

Card Meaning

The term "burnt offering" is based on the original Hebrew word "Olah" (pronounced *oh-law*) meaning "ascending," or "going upward into the smoke." The particular offering was often based on a person's social standing; the larger the animal sacrificed, the more they could afford to give as tribute. In the Ten of Swords, the chicken has become the symbolic burnt offering. The number ten denotes the end of one important cycle in life, and the beginning of another one. The chicken greets the dawn, but darkness always comes, but then, so does the next dawn. It represents the circle of life. A life is darkened and a light is transferred.

The Ten of Swords screams, "It's over!" There is no uncertainty in this ending. The chicken, or one cycle of life, is in the garbage. Following true to the entire suit of Swords, this is a painful ending. It seems that no important lessons can be learned without anger and disillusionment. This is, in part, because the nature of this suit is to analyze all situations, thereby trying to create a world of logic and fact that denies the messy creations built on feelings and intuition. Emotional realities will always be somewhat of a shock, and the pain will be very real, and difficult to explain away.

When you draw this card in a reading, you should breathe a sigh of relief because it is over. There is no guesswork involved and now is the time to start the healing process. This card can pertain to a relationship, a job, or the actual death of a loved one, person, or pet.

The good news in this card is that you are part of the natural rhythm of life, and the next dawn always comes, and the rooster will crow.

Kitchen Wisdom

"Self sacrifice? But it is precisely the self that cannot and must not be sacrificed."
~Ayn Rand, *The Fountainhead*

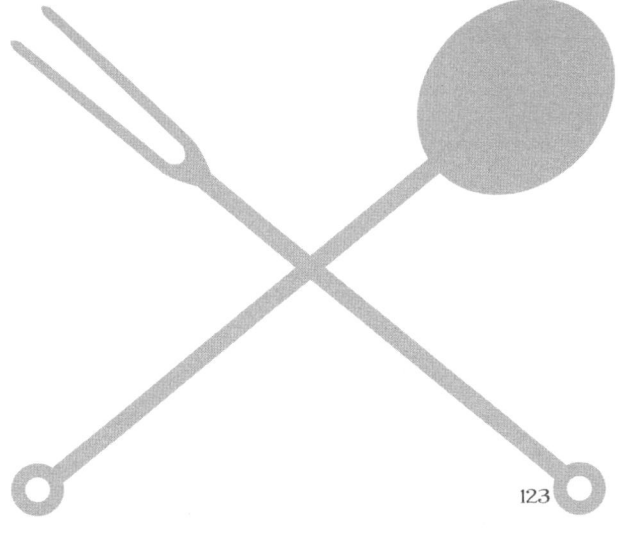

Page of Swords

A sudden gust of wind pushes open the kitchen window, allowing the stormy elements to invade the room. A young man dressed in a trench coat, busy at his midnight prying, does not seem to notice the raindrops or the leaves. Even though the wind further rustles open the pages of a notebook and swirls the water out of a pan, the Page of Swords is undeterred. He is on a fact-finding mission, and must know the secrets of the kitchen. He holds a knife loosely in one hand, and there is evidence of a carrot that he has been practicing on beside an open computer.

Key Elements

Page: All Pages are traditionally considered to be messengers of some kind. They do not necessarily have to represent real people, or even young people, but they bring to a reading the spirit or attitude of their particular suit. The Page of Swords signifies intellectual curiosity. Swords are associated with the element of air, and represent mental acuity, and pages approach problem solving from a rational rather than emotional perspective. They are excellent, if somewhat relentless, communicators as they are always asking, "why?"

Trench Coat: To a youthful imagination, the trench coat is an essential wardrobe element for any self-respecting agent of espionage. It has been well documented in countless spy novels and movies. The coat represents this Page's intellectual insatiability, along with his childlike love of games and secrets. He has a hard time removing this vintage spy-ware, and has been known to use it as a bathrobe.

Card Meaning

All Pages are associated with the element earth, and conjure images of seeds that have been planted in fertile soil. The Page of Swords is earth in the suit of Air. Even though the oxygen in the air is essential for the growth of seedlings, the wind that blows over them can damage their progress. This is one explanation for the inherent double-edged nature that follows the suit of Swords.

The stormy weather reflects the tumultuous nature of this young man. His thoughts seem to come at rapid fire and fall in many directions, just like the wind-blown leaves. He represents a gatherer of information, and is very comfortable with technology and every form of communication. Even though he has the grounding earth energy, his youthful body is often at odds with his analytical mind. He brings a feeling of tension and mild conflict to a reading.

When you are visited by this messenger, expect the rain clouds to follow. The Page does not bring bad news; he just brings to light a new series of facts and information. They can cause conflict if dealt with in an aggressive manner.

The shadow side of this card is the secret nature of the Page. He loves to know things about people, as it is all part of information gathering. Be cognizant about gossiping and try not to spread rumors whether they are true or not.

Kitchen Wisdom

Information can be clinical with no conflict attached to it.
It is how it's dealt with that can create the issues.

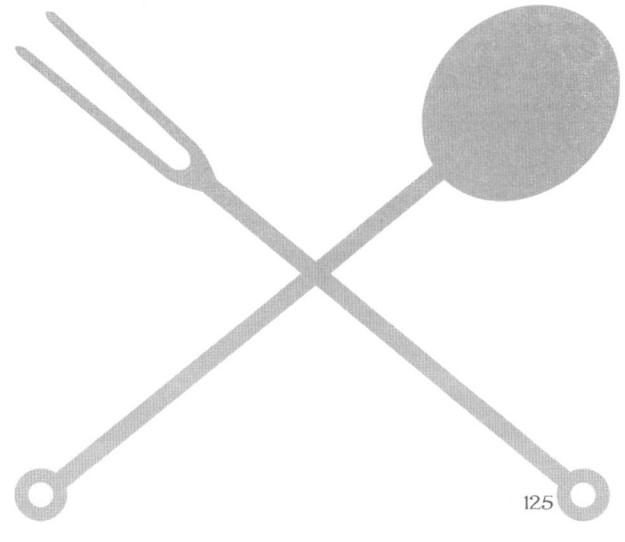

Knight of Swords

A young man is busy at work in the kitchen. He is staring straight ahead with a determined look on his face. He holds a cleaver in his upraised hand as if about to do battle with the vegetables on the chopping block. His cloak is blowing in the breeze from the open window, and the steam from the bubbling pots drift outside to mingle with the gathering storm clouds. There is a white stallion in a rampant position painted on his shirt. This Knight of Swords (for that is who he is) is lost in some idealistic daydream, and is not looking down towards the task at hand. One worries about both the fate of the food and his fingers.

Key Elements

Knight: A member of the warrior class that represents action and courage. They are the *traditional defenders of the realm*. Knights are identified as possessing the extreme qualities of their suits. They are associated with movement, either physical or intuitive, and are therefore seen as catalysts for change. This Knight represents the suit of Swords, which is associated with the element air. He is intelligent, headstrong, and an idealistic champion of causes. He is known to be very self-assured and very caustic in his criticisms of others. Although he is considered emotionally aloof, he will rush to the aid of anyone in distress.

Horse: A symbol of strength, victory, and freedom. The color of the horse represents the nature of the Knight. This horse is a white stallion, forelegs raised high and ready to charge. This speaks to the purity of the Knight's intentions. He believes in duty and honor, and despite his intellectual prowess, he is a romantic at heart. This horse will take the Knight into the thick of battle with no thought as to safety or consequence. "Fools rush in where angels fear to tread."

Card Meaning

The Knight of Swords is about facing conflict, as if you were going into battle. The energy of this card is based on youthful idealism as well as a strong sense of intellectual superiority. It is a good card to get in a reading if there is a difficult situation that needs to be resolved because the Knight of Swords would not waste time worrying over it. He would tell you to research your facts and then march right in and settle the matter. In a case for resolving conflict, you will need the Knight's self-confidence along with his frank and direct approach.

If you get this card and recognize such a person in your life, you might want to think carefully about becoming too attached. This Knight is rather egotistical, and has a tendency to move on when he becomes bored.

The shadow side to this card is that the Knight does get bored. He requires a great deal of intellectual stimulation, and has not matured enough to channel it towards a single goal. He will always be looking for the next cause to champion. This is a good kind of person to have if you are trying to run a fundraiser, but a bad person to get into an argument with.

Kitchen Wisdom

If something has to go on the chopping block,
vegetables are a better choice than heads.

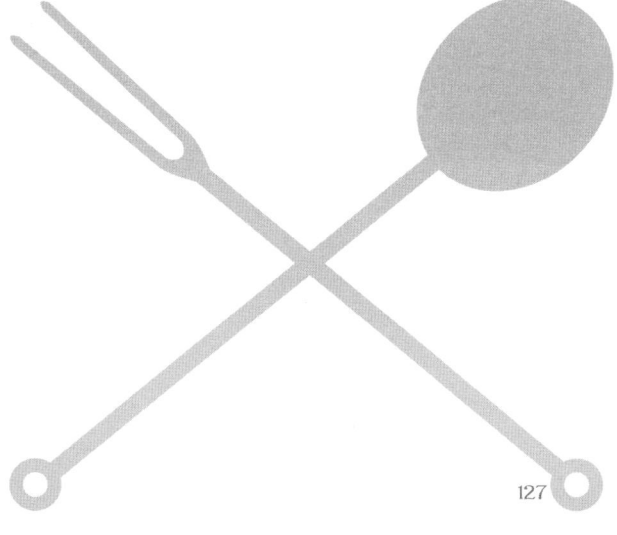

Queen of Swords

The Queen of Swords is disguised as a food critic. She is sitting with an imperious air at a newly opened sushi restaurant. She has a direct gaze, and her head seems to be so full of knowledge that her slender neck is having trouble supporting it. She has a stopwatch beside her to time the waiters as she rates their level of efficiency. A pen hovers over a check list as she judges the food for presentation, taste, freshness, and price. The obsequious waiters and the large sword on the table have taken this image from the land of reality to the realm of symbolism.

Key Elements

Pen: The phrase "The pen is mightier than the sword," was originally attributed to Edward Bulwer-Lyttton, and has come to mean that thinking and writing have more influence over people and events than the use of force or violence. This is interesting as the suit of Swords is associated with the element air and represents the mind and communication. It also speaks to the rational and logical way we go about making decisions. It is a suit that acknowledges facts over emotions. In Tarot, the pen and the sword are very closely aligned.

Sword: Typically, a sword is a symbol of masculinity and represents armed force. In the world of Tarot, the sword represents the ability to cut to the heart of a matter. To cut away the fluff of emotions and expose the hard core of fact and logic. Swords are double-edged, and in this way they have the ability to help and to hurt you. The suit of Swords is known for its suffering ,as lessons learned are often painful, and knowledge never comes easily. The pen has become the sword, and wounds caused by words are often longer lasting and harder to heal than those caused by an actual weapon.

King of Swords

Judgment has been pronounced. The sushi is good. The King of Swords is the only King in the Tarot Court that is on equal terms with his partner in matters of governing and issuing verdicts. They are both depicted as having assumed the roles of critics and the success of each restaurant rides on their authority. The King is shown making the traditional *thumbs-up* gesture, which has come to be recognized as a sign of approval. A chef is standing in the background, his head bowed in deference, with his knife resting against his shoulder in a gesture of humility and respect.

A pair of glasses and a rolled up newspaper lie in front of the King, symbols of his dedication to knowledge and learning. They also imply that he likes to eat alone and does not enjoy interruptions.

Key Elements

Thumbs-up Gesture: Anthropologists consider the development of the opposable thumb as the vital evolutionary step that separates man from the animals. "The thumb is to the hand, what the hand is to the brain." Classical Romans and Greeks regarded the thumb as a phallic symbol, and considered it a symbol of fertility. In palmistry, the character and karmic potential of a person can be determined by the size, color, and shape of the thumb. Mudras are hand gestures that have symbolic meaning in both Hindu and Buddhist religions. There are over a hundred different mudras and each tell a different tale or teach a specific lesson. In Hindu religious dancing, there are twenty-eight single-hand mudras. The tenth mudra looks just like the *thumbs-up* sign, a clenched fist with a vertically extended thumb, and it is performed for health and wealth. There is debate among scholars as to the meaning of thumb gestures in the Roman amphitheaters, but it has been generally proven that a gladiator would not have been happy to see a series of upraised thumbs in the crowds, as this meant his certain death. The debate continues as to whether the thumb was to be hidden or pointed sideways for leniency.

CARD MEANING

All the Tarot queens are associated with the element water; this makes them very knowledgeable about the emotional aspects of life. The Queen of Swords is also associated with the element air. She is water of air, meaning that she can understand emotions and is not immune to their power and she has the ability to judge impartially without being influenced by them. She has the reputation for being rather ice-like in her demeanor.

This queen prizes intelligence. She has integrity and is not afraid of speaking the truth, even though it might not be the popular opinion of the day. The Queen of Swords is fair in her judgment and does not seek to wound; she says nothing with malicious intent. The water aspect of her character allows her to use tact and diplomacy while still speaking the truth.

When you draw this card in a reading, you must not be put off by her severe gaze. You will be needing her energy and strength of character as your opinion will soon be called upon. Do not take the easy way out and say what you think people want to hear, but instead, speak the truth as you know it, straight from the heart.

The shadow side of this card comes from being in the position of judging others. You can become harsh and jaded, and life will be lonely. If you find this happening, soften your gaze and judge with compassion.

KITCHEN WISDOM

"To err is human; to forgive, divine."
~Alexander Pope

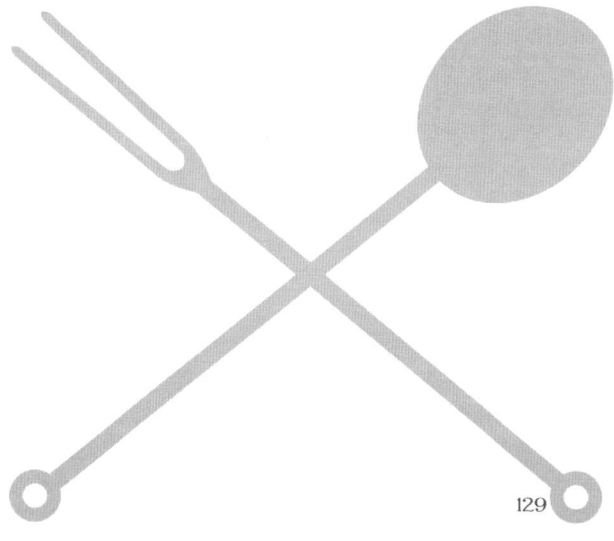

Card Meaning

Arete (pronounced *ah-ree-tay*) is a Greek term meaning "living up to one's highest human potential." In terms of chivalry, arete is the achievement of the greatest good and highest virtue obtained by the fusion of reason with compassion. These attributes defines the King of Swords, reason and compassion. As a King, he represents the power and success of his suit. All Kings are associated with the element air, which allows them intellectual prowess and the ability to make decisions in a fair and rational manner. The suit of Swords is also based on the element air. This King is air of air. His natural tendencies are towards a lofty idealism. He favors facts over emotions and is known for his skill in strategy and planning. The maturity of his years has allowed him to temper his stern nature with a more understanding outlook towards humanity.

When you draw this card in a reading, the King is telling you to be objective in your reasoning. There are likely to be issues involving the discernment of truth and the passing of impartial judgment in your life. It might be time to seek the help of an expert if there are potential legal struggles involved. This is a somber card, in that no one likes to be in front of a judge, but at least you know the ruling will be fair.

If you need to borrow this King's energy, you will be in the position of deciding the outcome of a situation. This is the time to be detached from your emotions and let the facts speak for themselves.

The shadow side of this card is that the emotions have become completely blocked off. You have to remember the compassion aspect of the King, and balance will be obtained.

Kitchen Wisdom

Equality and courtesy do not have to be mutually exclusive.

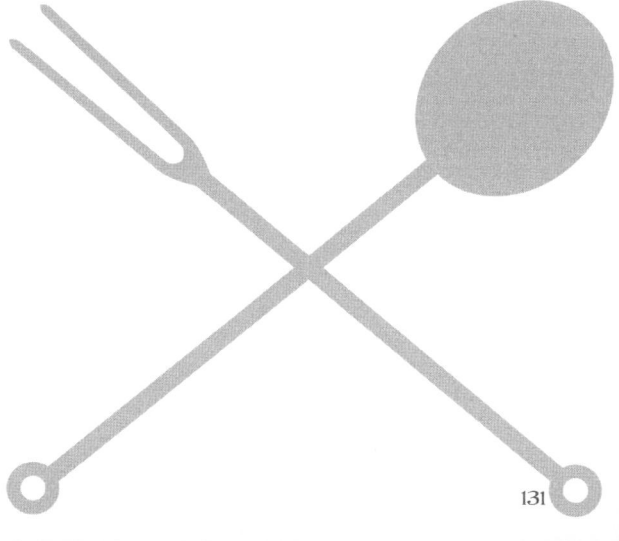

Ace of Pentacles

An outstretched hand is holding an apple that has been cut in half horizontally. It lies in the center of a yellow plate that has a pentagram inscribed on it. The hand hovers over a round table that is accompanied by a single chair. On the table, a bright pink ribbon remains tied over a gift box whose wrapping paper, covered in a rose pattern, lies crumpled around it. A golden shaft of sunlight illuminates the scene, creating another triangular point that leads the viewer over the table, across the floor, and out the door to a winding path leading to the distant hills.

Key Elements

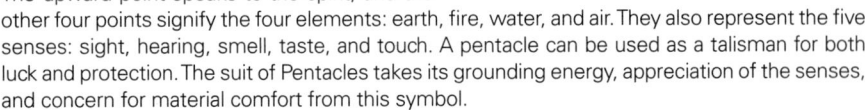

Pentacle: A pentagram is a five-pointed star that represents the five or quintessential elements. The upward point speaks to the spirit, and the other four points signify the four elements: earth, fire, water, and air. They also represent the five senses: sight, hearing, smell, taste, and touch. A pentacle can be used as a talisman for both luck and protection. The suit of Pentacles takes its grounding energy, appreciation of the senses, and concern for material comfort from this symbol.

Apple: An apple that has been cut horizontally reveals a pentacle, star-like shape. The number of seeds found inside can be used for divination purposes. The apple itself is rich with symbolic meaning that includes knowledge, fertility, desire, and even temptation and discord.

Gift Box: A pretty package wrapped in seductive pink ribbon. The outer wrapping paper has been removed, but the box remains unopened. This is the gift that is offered by the Ace of Pentacles. It is potential in its purest form. What you find in that box has everything to do with how you accept generosity. In this case, the box must be opened, implying an action must be taken in order to manifest the bounty of the suit of Pentacles.

Card Meaning

The Ace is the first card in the suit of Pentacles, and therefore sets the tone for the rest of the suit. Aces are viewed as gifts, and the disembodied hand that is providing the offering implies that the moment is fleeting and must be quickly grasped and acted on. Aces are the power players of the Tarot deck, and, in a reading, act as trump cards, upstaging even the Major Arcana.

The Ace of Pentacles offers all the generosity and bounty of this earth-based suit. The worldly pleasures, the sensual comforts, and the material gain are all inside that box waiting to be opened. When you draw this card in a reading, a new beginning leading to success is before you. As with all new beginnings, a change of direction is involved. It may be as simple as accepting the gift, or it may require you to act quickly in order to find the gift. A financial windfall, or a new job offer might present themselves.

In this card, a left hand holding a plate is emerging from the left side of the page. The left is considered to be the feminine, or passive, side and contains yin energy, which is best used for accepting and receiving. The accepting of the apple, or gift of knowledge, requires no action other than to receive. It is what happens next, what you make of the gift, that requires the action.

The shadow side of this card lies in not reciprocating generosity. You have two hands, one to give and one to receive. Using only the yin energy can detract from the power of the gift and your ventures will be less successful.

Kitchen Wisdom

Take what is offered, but remember to say, "Thank you."

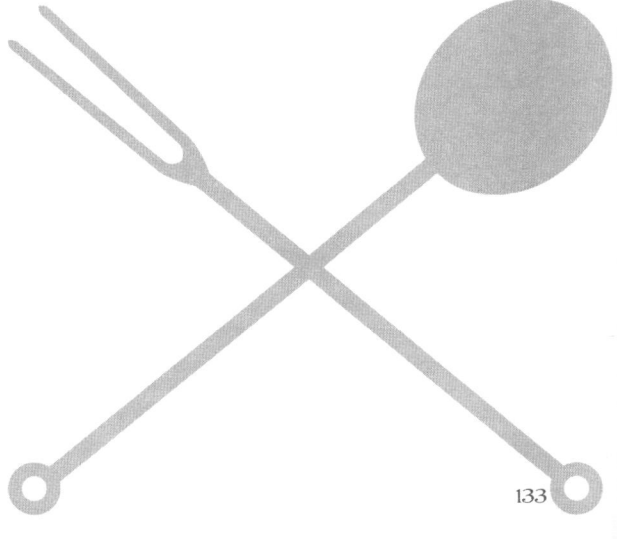

Two of Pentacles

A woman is shown standing with one foot firmly on the ground, while the other is raised as she attempts to balance a broom that has two buckets of water hanging from it. She holds an apple in one upraised hand and an orange in the other. There is a lemniscate loosely wrapped around both of her arms. Water is everywhere. It is pouring out of the painting behind her; it is falling into one of the buckets, which in turn is causing a pool to collect on the floor. Despite the chaos, she looks serene. There are paintbrushes in her uniform pocket and bags full of groceries on the floor. She represents every woman who has ever tried to have a creative outlet, hold down a job, feed a family, and clean a house. She is a multi-tasking queen.

Key Elements

Lemniscate: The image of a figure eight on its side is also known as the infinity symbol. It represents continuous motion and the endless and eternal nature of energy. The lemniscate describes an unending continuum with no beginning or end. Therefore, when this symbol appears in a card it means that the actions we take now will affect future outcomes. There are consequences to be considered. Important decisions need to be made and careful attention should be paid to the situation.

Water: The source of life. An ocean responds to the tides; the water ebbs and flows in continuous motion. Water can cleanse and nurture. It can represent a healing or soothing of the emotions just as it can describe confusion and uncertainty as we struggle against the pulling tides.

Water in a bucket is said to represent good fortune, but stagnant water is a sign of fortunes gone away. Two buckets symbolize a destiny that involves serving others.

Broom: This has many connotations. It can represent domesticity as it is used to clean both home and hearth. It can be a symbol of witchcraft, and has even been used as part of marriage ceremonies, representing fidelity. To dream of a broom indicates that you need to mentally clear a path and pay attention to what you are sweeping up. In this card, the broom is also being used as a yoke to carry the two buckets of water. A yoke is a sign of oppression, which is another warning to heed.

Card Meaning

There is a saying, "You can't compare apples to oranges," meaning that there are two separate issues that cannot be judged the same way. This is the dilemma of our heroine. She is trying to balance opposing forces. The very nature of the pentacle suit is to be connected to the earth, grounded and stable. In this card, the water element provides a sense of the intangible. It speaks of travel and movement. One must be very flexible in order to balance these juxtapositions.

In a reading, this card describes coping with at least two separate situations at once. It requires energy and grace in order to be effective. There will come a time when a decision will have to be made as to which direction to focus on. This card asks you to examine the boats in the picture. Are you charting the right course? Any action requires careful thought and deliberation as finances are usually involved with the outcome. Consider what baggage you are bringing onboard and also who your passengers will be.

Kitchen Wisdom

You can't do everything. Stop procrastinating and make a decision, or the ship of opportunity will sail without you.

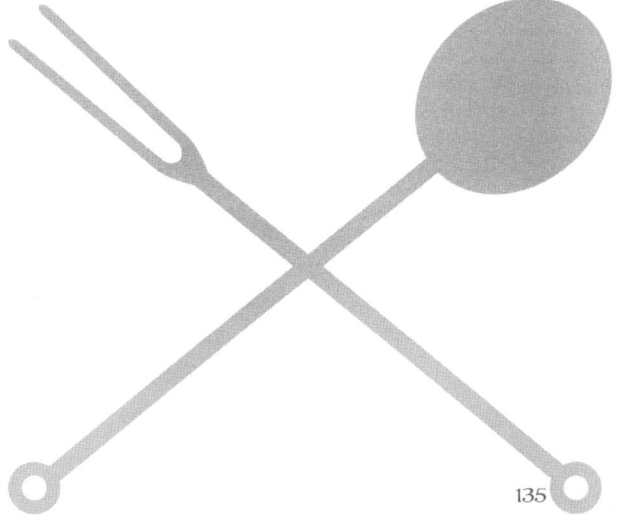

Three of Pentacles

A woman is seated at a restaurant table. She holds an open menu and raises her face towards the waiter who is standing beside her. He holds a pad and pen in front of him ready to take her order. A chef, who is busy making pizzas behind the counter, pauses in his work to watch them. All three are connected by a triangle of light. Their collective arms seem to form a pattern, similar to that of spokes on a wheel.

Key Elements

Triangle: A triangle is one of the most fundamental of geometric symbols and is inseparable from the number 3. In ancient Egypt, a triangle was recognized as a symbol for love, balance, creativity, and intelligence. In numerological terms, it has left the confines of the couple and now describes the nature of the group. It is the birthing of wisdom and also speaks of balance and creativity. There is no way to see a triangle, or the number 3, without considering the tripartite nature of the world: heavens, earth, waters; beginning, middle, end; body, soul, spirit; past, present, future; birth, life, death; and even the cycles of the moon, waxing, waning and full. We are all connected to this sacred geometry which provides the harmony and balance to our lives.

Arch: This often represents the vault of the sky. Passing through an arch is symbolic of rebirth. It represents leaving the old behind, and entering the new.

Apron: It is a garment associated with work and craftsmanship.

Card Meaning

The Three of Pentacles celebrates the group over the individual. It is about the nature of cooperation. As a member of the Pentacle suit, it is strongly associated with work, career, and finances. This card acknowledges that as individuals you have acquired certain skills, but in order to fulfill a dream or project, you must work within a group. This could mean going back to school for further education, or simply asking for help with a project. Persistence, determination, and effort can make a dream a reality.

The shadow side of this card warns against laziness and lack of ambition. You are only going to get as much as you give in this particular situation.

Kitchen Wisdom

You cannot succeed all by yourself. Mutual cooperation, involving a third party is needed to complete this venture. In the words of Alexander Dumas' three musketeers, "All for one and one for all!"

Four of Pentacles

In a narrow room, high above the ground, a woman stands in front of a padlocked cupboard. The chain is loosely draped through the door handles and, even though she cannot open the doors completely, she can easily pry them apart. She is adding a fourth jar of preserves to her carefully gathered hoard, but her position just as easily describes the removal of a precious jar.

On a nearby windowsill, a Magpie is sitting on its nest contemplating the shiny collection of stolen objects. Both the bird and the human are completely engrossed in their calculations and are ignoring the existence of the neighboring village with all its noisy needs and demands.

Key Elements

Four Jars of Preserves: Four is a number of wholeness and completion. It is a solid number that signifies a foundation of strength and stability. It is associated with the qualities of The Emperor in the Major Arcana. The pentacle labels on the jars associate them with heavy earth energy and therefore describe material concerns. The jars of preserves are also a play on the word "preserve" which means two separate things. The first is to protect, to keep something safe from harm or injury, and the second is to maintain, to keep something for a long time. In the case of fruit, it is to prevent decomposition. To protect and maintain is the logo for the Four of Pentacles.

Magpie: A bird that by its very nature is attracted to all the shiny things that belong to others. It has become a symbol of greed and avarice. In this card, it serves as a warning to not let the need to conserve become a need to hoard. It is also a way of stating that glittering objects are not always the most valuable, as in "fools gold." The magpie also acts as the villain in the card by representing the archetypal thief, and thus generating the cry, "Do not take what does not belong to you."

CARD MEANING

The Four of Pentacles, like all the Fours in the Minor Arcana, represents a solid foundation on which to build. It is the natures of their respective suits that call other issues into play. Since a pentagram represents the four elements along with the spirit, and the Pentacle suit represents a connection with the five senses, this card is heavily grounded and speaks to keeping and preserving what you have. When you draw this card in a reading, you are being asked to examine what it is that you are holding onto, and to question whether your grip is too loose or too tight.

If you are in a position of financial security, this card is preoccupied with keeping things from changing. If you are in a stable relationship, this card suggests that things might have come to a plateau; complacency does not allow for further growth and evolution. If you are trying to get to this level of establishment, the magpie warns that an anxious and grasping nature does not bring security.

As usual, the Tarot speaks to you about finding balance. The Four of Pentacles speaks to the differences between preserving something that is good with an eye towards future posterity versus clinging to something that you have accumulated because you fear that you will lose it if you relax your grip.

KITCHEN WISDOM

It is wise to put away preserves following a good harvest, but foolish if you try to save them through winter.

Five of Pentacles

A young child wearing a yellow raincoat stops in front of the window of a candy store. He is mesmerized by the tempting display of shapes and colors. He opens his arms wide with wonder, paying no attention to the falling rain. His mother has a firm grasp on his hand and is trying to pull him away. She is in a hurry, and has no intention of going inside the store. Neither of them notice that they are standing on a chalk drawing. It is an artist's rendition of a stained glass window that is already being destroyed as the colors bleed and run together from the pouring rain.

FIVE OF PENTACLES

Key Elements

Candy Store: We have all heard the expression, "Like a kid in a candy store," knowing it to mean that you are surrounded by such temptation that you don't know what to choose first. This child is outside the candy store unable to get in. All the pleasures of life are being withheld; at least that is what he feels. His childish mind is lured by the sheer display of excess that is in front of him and he resents being pulled away.

The candy behind the glass wall represents all those material possessions that we do not have. They are stacked up and on display, so we know that other people are getting those things and we feel even more bitter and resentful about our perceived poverty.

Chalk Drawing: The drawing of the five pentacles in a stained glass window is a bit of an oxymoron. Stained glass windows were created to beautify churches and symbolize religious faith. Unfortunately, those windows were often commissioned by rich patrons and symbolized that individual's social standing in the church, rather than their spiritual growth. Pentacles are a Pagan symbol that would not make likely additions to a church window. In this card, they also represent the suit of Pentacles, which is about material gain and the appreciation of all things sensual.

The beauty of the drawing is going unnoticed by the mother and child. One is distracted by the display inside the store and the other is in a hurry to get out of the rain. The irony in the combination of material and spiritual symbolism is lost on them. The drawing is melting, showing that a thing of beauty is not forever.

CARD MEANING:

The Five of Pentacles, on initial inspection, is about being left out in the rain, and not getting what you want. It is a card of dejection and hopelessness. Or is it? The number 5 represents restlessness and action that together lead to new life experiences. It is also the number of The Hierophant, the fifth card of the Major Arcana. The Hierophant teaches us to appreciate secular activity, and to get a solid foundation in traditional values before branching out and developing a new set of experiences.

This card is about not paying attention to what is under your feet. In other words, your attention is focused on what is unattainable and you are not seeing what you already have. If the strong foundation is there, you will easily find what you need. It is also about refocusing your energies towards a more spiritual and less materialistic outcome.

When you draw this card in a reading, you are being asked if you are being like that child in front of the candy display. You are to revisit your motives and to decide if it is more important to do one of three things. Walk away and get out of the rain; stop what you are doing and look at the beauty around you; or go into the store and buy some candy, already!

The shadow side to this card lies in believing that all that candy is meant for others. It implies a feeling of self pity and victimization. This is to be guarded against as these qualities are both unattractive and self defeating.

KITCHEN WISDOM

Sometimes life gets complicated, and you have to go back to the basics.

Six of Pentacles

A man sits, balancing on the low branch of an apple tree, his feet dangling in front of him. With his right arm, he is reaching up towards a bird's nest searching for the eggs. With his left arm he is handing one of the apples from an overfilled bag to a woman waiting below the tree. Kneeling forward on the ground is a boy gathering up all the fruit that has fallen. He is piling them into a box that is filling rapidly.

Key Elements

Apple: This fruit is rich with symbolism and has a long association with knowledge, temptation, and immortality. The fruit can be viewed as coinage in a bartering situation. In this card, the apples symbolize generosity. Apples are closely related to the Pentacle suit because when one is cut sideways, the seed pods have a five-starred, pentacle shape.

Hands: Traditionally, because the hands are thought of as extensions of the brain, they are given the same characteristics. The right hand is considered to contain the masculine qualities of logic and assertiveness. It is the yang component, and used for giving, which is an active deed. The left hand embodies the female, or yin, characteristics. It is said to be passive, emotional, and open to receiving. In some societies, it is considered impolite and ungrateful to accept a gift with one hand only; both should be extended together, sides touching and palms open. Hands that are held together, palms touching, show respect and humility. How you relate to the hands in this card is key to what the meaning holds for you. Are they taking, stealing, giving, receiving, accepting, or simply collecting?

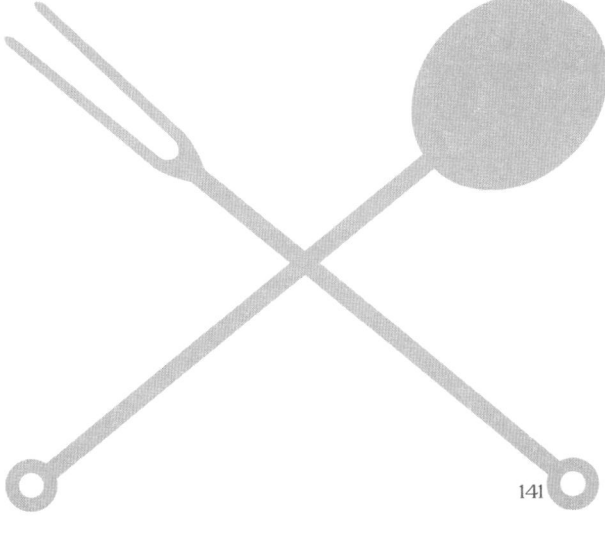

Card Meaning

Like all of the sixes, the Six of Pentacles is primarily about balance. Pentacles represent the element earth and are therefore strongly associated with bodily concerns and finances. These are the grounding influences that create reliability and stability. This card is about the shifts that occur in balancing these needs. Those that have must give, and those that need will receive.

As is often seen in Tarot, there is a duality to every act. There is both a light and shadow side to the act of giving. Sometimes charity may be misguided if it does nothing to empower the one receiving it, but instead creates even more dependence. On the other hand, charity is needed to alleviate the suffering and misery of those less fortunate. What becomes important is the intention behind the act.

When you draw this card in a reading, it is time to consider what is out of balance in your life. If you are having financial difficulties, you should open your mind to receiving material gain. Give what you have to give; time and energy are often worth more than money. You will find yourself materially rewarded. If you are feeling prosperous, this is a good time to share the wealth; you will be rewarded with something that you need.

The danger to this card lies in becoming too focused on material gratification, or becoming greedy. This card warns you not to incur more debt or to spend irresponsibly. Again, balance is the key.

Kitchen Wisdom

If the right hand doesn't know what the left hand is doing,
it is time to put them both together.

Seven of Pentacles

The summer has come to an end and the harvest is being gathered. An impatient young woman stands in her kitchen. She is looking at her watch trying to decide what to do. She has a large knife in her hand, knowing that the tomatoes lying in front of her need to be dealt with. She is looking at the old-fashioned stock pot and thinking how long it would take for these fruit to simmer into a sauce. The microwave door is open, and light is spilling out, illuminating her open purse and spilled coins. She is debating whether to take the time to cook the fruit slowly, or to use a faster and more expedient method of completing her task. The coins and purse suggest that for this woman, time is money.

Key Elements

Coins: Pentacles are strongly associated with the element earth. They have been called many things in different decks, such as discs or coins. In this card, the seven coins represent the financial aspect of the suit of Pentacles. They are symbolic of material wealth, or the lack of it (as seen with the empty wallet), and speak to the issue of values. Coins raise questions about how to spend money wisely, and also how to determine personal priorities. What you choose to spend money on tells you what your values are. There is also the issue of spending money or spending time. In some situations, you have to invest both time and money in order to succeed.

Tomatoes: The "Alchemical Properties of Food" describes tomatoes as being called "love apples" when they were first introduced to Europe. They were used to not only solicit romance, but to repel negative influences. To dream of tomatoes in any form is a happy omen, meaning that success and contentment are coming your way. In this card, they are symbolic of a body of work that has been completed, but has not yet paid off financially.

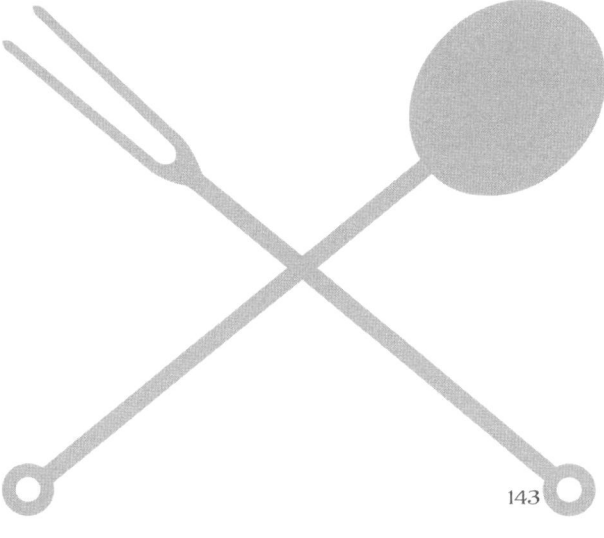

Card Meaning

The Seven of Pentacles is about assessing past achievements. The number seven speaks to problem solving, thought, and consciousness. Now that there is something to show for your efforts, you are at a crossroads as to how to proceed. This card takes its lead from the seventh archetype of the Major Arcana, The Chariot. The charioteer is moving forward by the way he controls the reins of his horses. This card is about controlling your path to success. It is tempting to be impatient and to take the easy way, but in the long run, will that be wise?

When you draw this card in a reading, you are being asked to consider what it is that you value. The coins in the card speak to your potential and ask you whether you are going to barter profitably or not. They also ask you to take a close look at your present priorities and decide if you need to be patient and give more of your time, or if you need to take control and make more money. It is the age old dilemma—time versus money. This card is implying that success will come with patience, and the shadow side of this is that "haste makes waste," but only you know what direction you need to steer your chariot towards. The bottom line is not to rush towards a decision, but to choose thoughtfully.

Kitchen Wisdom

"Whether it's the best of times or the worst of times,
it's the only time we've got."

~Art Buchwald

Eight of Pentacles

A triangle of light floods through the windowpane, finding its way through a large pentacle that is propped against it. A sleepy town lies in the distance beyond a sunlit field. The baker with his head down is ignoring the bucolic scene in front of him. He is bent forward, leaning towards his task of rolling out the next piece of dough. There is an empty pan on the windowsill, waiting to join the others that are stacked high on the shelves behind him.

Key Elements

Pentacle: A five-pointed star, with one upward point, that symbolizes the quintessential nature of man. The upward point represents the spirit, and the other four represent the elements: earth, fire, water, and air. A pentacle with a circle around it symbolizes closure and protection, while an open pentagram denotes active participation and a willingness to solve problems through conflict. In the Minor Arcana, the suit of Pentacles is related to the element earth and represents the five senses: sight, hearing, touch, smell, and taste. The baker is fully involved in all of his senses, which are dedicated to his appointed task.

Eight Pies: The number 8 is said to be the perfect number. It symbolizes cosmic order and balance as it describes an infinity sign that is laid on its side. It is often associated with prosperity and hard work. In this card, there are seven pies that have been completed, and one remaining pan sits empty, waiting to be filled. They represent the goals that have been achieved while working on a long-term project. The effort is not yet over, but success will soon be realized. There is also the concept of perfection to deal with as it is an issue that can hinder forward motion.

Rolling Dough: Dough is a slang term for money. To be rolling in dough means to have a lot of money. The significance of this visual play on words is that hard work will result in financial success.

CARD MEANING

The Eight of Pentacles is about single-minded dedication to a difficult project. It involves a prolonged period of learning and apprenticeship that is about to come to an end. The emphasis of this card lies in perseverance. You create your own success; it is not freely given to you.

When you draw this card in a reading, you are being asked to continue with your efforts, even though you may be tired and ready for distraction. It usually involves education that will lead to job improvement and financial rewards. If you are not currently involved in schooling of some kind, it speaks to a self-actualizing goal—sort of like creating a Tarot deck. Your back hurts; you bend forward, nose to the grindstone, because it takes that kind of focus and determination to get the job done.

The shadow side to this card is twofold. You can be so focused on achieving your goals that you lose sight of "the forest for the trees," and do not clearly see the big picture. You keep rolling out the dough when the pans are all filled. The other enemy is perfection. Is it possible to achieve? If you keep making the perfect crust, it becomes the status quo. We come back to the purpose of the number eight and that is to achieve balance. Balance your hard work and efforts with a firm grasp on reality and you will be rolling in the dough.

KITCHEN WISDOM

These pies are not going to make themselves!

Nine of Pentacles

It is a moment of utter bliss. On this beautiful summer day, a woman is luxuriating in the warmth of the sun; all her senses are satisfied. She has chosen to place her chair beside a garden bed where she can smell the fresh grass, hear the birds chirping, feel the cat purring, and taste the fresh cold water and sweet bites of chocolate. She has put her book aside for a moment and the weight of it is a pleasant reminder of the pleasure that awaits when she opens her eyes. She inhales deeply, eyes still closed, in a silent prayer of gratitude.

Key Elements

Red Bird: Because of their ability to claim both the heavens and earth as their natural domain, birds have been seen as symbols for the human soul. They represent freedom and spiritual transition. In this card, the red bird is a reminder that moments of beauty are brief and can easily take flight. This little bird is a gift.

Orange Cat: There is longstanding tradition of cats in mythology and folklore. They have come to symbolize a deeper understanding of our natural world. They are a blend of the physical, spiritual, psychic, and sensual, and serve as reminders that one can never truly understand the mysterious. Orange is a happy color. It is the color of the second chakra, located near the womb and related to joy and creativity.

Chocolate: A symbol of care, love, and life. Chocolate as a gift is associated with passion and sensuality. In this card, it serves as a reminder that the greatest gift that we can give ourselves is an appreciation for the pleasures of life.

Card Meaning

The Nine of Pentacles is about self-empowerment. In numerology, nine represents the end of a cycle and the attainment of what you set out to achieve. The suit of Pentacles represents the physical manifestation of an idea. It is strongly associated with the element earth and, therefore, with the gaining of creature comforts, all of which serve to fulfill the needs of all five physical senses. This card speaks to the moment of success, when you feel that you have finally reaped the benefits of a long and difficult struggle. In many cases, the rewards are financial, but in this particular card the emphasis is on the wealth that comes with emotional contentment.

The Nine of Pentacles is closely aligned with The Hermit, the ninth card of the Major Arcana. Whereas The Hermit has turned his back on the material needs of society in order to find a higher truth, the woman in this card has secluded herself in order to appreciate her independence.

When you draw this card in a reading, you are being asked to consider what makes you happy. More than likely, you will realize that at this particular moment in time you have everything that you need and that you are rich indeed. If you are not content with your situation, this card asks you to consider the reasons why not, and gives you permission to go and get some chocolate. It is time to give yourself a present.

The shadow side to this card occurs when the isolation becomes a barrier to letting others close to you.

Kitchen Wisdom

Chocolate makes everything better.
Trust me on this one.

Ten of Pentacles

The goose is standing on the table proudly spreading its wings because it has laid another golden egg. The happy couple hold hands as they marvel at their good fortune. Not only do they have each other, but they have a steady and reliable source of income to provide financial security for the years ahead. The children in the background are busy collecting the golden eggs and putting them in a basket. However, not everyone is impressed by this talented goose. The dog is quite happy to sit beside his mistress while she pats his head. He thinks the goose is a big loudmouthed braggart, fit only for the Sunday roast, as it brings no love and loyalty to the table. In the background an axe is lodged in the stump of a tree, bringing a somewhat somber note to the scene.

Key Elements

Ten Pentacles: Ten is the number of completion, associated with the need to start something new. It signifies that the goals that one set out to accomplish have been achieved, and that this is the period of tying up loose ends, or putting affairs in order before beginning the next phase of life. Pentacles are associated with the earth element and are, therefore, strongly related to creature comforts and a fulfilling of the five senses. The tenth card in the Major Arcana is The Wheel of Fortune, which suggests that the wheel is turning and success is now available, either in the form of an unexpected windfall, or as the result of investments paying off after years of struggle.

The Goose: The goose that laid the golden egg is a parable about the pitfalls of greed and the desire for quick rewards. In Aesop's tale (one version of this life lesson), a farmer and his wife had a goose that laid one golden egg every morning. In time, they became dissatisfied with this slow accumulation of eggs and thought that the goose must have a giant amount of gold inside it in order to keep producing the eggs. They killed the goose and were sadly disappointed to find that it was just an ordinary bird with no hidden gold. Their greed caused them to lose both the goose and the eggs.

CARD MEANING

The Ten of Pentacles is about family and prosperity. It is a very positive card that implies financial success in which the whole family will benefit, whether it be in the form of new possessions, an inheritance, or a career advancement for the main provider. This card also speaks to the end of a cycle, meaning that this accumulation of wealth will end if it is not invested wisely and passed on to future generations.

Although material wealth is certainly an important aspect of life, it is not everything. When you draw this card in a reading, you are being asked to look at everything that is being shown, including the dog, the goose, and the axe.

This card is acting as a bit of a cautionary tale. It is saying yes, be happy with good fortune, but do not forget that it brings about the end of one cycle. In order not to go backwards or fall off The Wheel of Fortune, you need to think of future generations, and realize that wealth is also a state of mind.

The shadow side to this card is, of course, greed and the short-sighted thrill of instant gratification.

KITCHEN WISDOM

The person who has everything he or she needs is wealthy indeed.

Page of Pentacles

A young man stands at a kitchen table. He is studiously measuring out ingredients, concentrating on the task at hand. He wears a jaunty red feather in his cap that contradicts the serious expression on his face. On the table is a piggy bank standing on top of a pile of paper money.

Behind our young entrepreneur is an open window through which curtains are gently blowing. There is a flower pot of geraniums on the windowsill and the view is of plowed fields and distant mountains.

Key Elements

Page: All Pages are traditionally considered to be messengers of some kind. They do not necessarily have to be real people, or even young people, but they bring to a reading the spirit or attitude of their particular suit. All Pages represent the element earth; symbolically, this is where seeds are planted and new growth begins. The Page of Pentacles represents earthly things such as the five senses, health, and finance.

Piggy Bank: The name is derived from the old English word "pygge," which was an alluvial substance used in the building of small containers. These were often used for storing valuables. They have now become a means of teaching children the value of money. The lesson being, "Save all your coins and when the bank is full you can buy something special."

Plowed Fields: The phrase, "As we sow, so shall we reap" is represented by these fertile fields. If one is careful in the preparation and nurturing of a project, the rewards will be bountiful.

Red Feather: Red is an emotionally charged color representing passion. A feather is light, and connected to the element air bringing thoughts of wind and flight. This combination tempers serious emotion with a sense of lightheartedness.

Card Meaning

When we are visited by the Page of Pentacles in a reading, we are being asked to listen carefully to advice regarding the starting of a new venture. It is usually financial in nature even though the issues might be emotional or health related. This Page gathers all the information prior to making a decision. He carefully lays the groundwork and deliberately goes over the pros and cons. As the Page also represents youth and playfulness, we are warned not to take ourselves too seriously, but rather have faith that whatever effort we put into a task will be rewarded in kind.

The shadow side of this card warns against the placing of too much importance on material wealth. The piggy bank is funny, and it is an inadequate container for serious finances. This card tells us that rewards are in the future, so we must be patient and pay attention to what our senses are asking. Does it look, feel, smell, sound, and taste right? Listen to your internal messenger.

Kitchen Wisdom

A gourmet meal can be created with simple items.
It is the freshness and preparation that matters.

Knight of Pentacles

An earnest looking young man, who is wearing a flowing cloak over his uniform, holds a pizza box open as if in offering. Behind him lie acres of plowed fields. A dark horse is standing by the edge of the road looking curiously at the Knight's delivery van, which happens to be the same dark color.

Key Elements

Knight: A member of the warrior class that represents action and courage, the traditional defenders of the realm. In Tarot terms, Knights are identified with the extreme qualities of their individual suits. They are associated with movement, whether physical or intuitive, and are, therefore, seen as the catalysts of change. This Knight embodies none of these aggressive characteristics. He is seen far away from his horse, which is also not moving. He is a symbol of steadfast reliability, a slow-moving and hard-working man who takes his responsibilities to heart.

Horse: A symbol of strength, victory, nobility, and freedom. The color of the horse represents the nature of the Knight. This one is dark and somber, symbolizing the seriousness of his intentions and the heaviness of his burden. This horse, like his knight, is not an action figure. He represents a more plodding and methodical approach to situations and will not be distracted by superficial concerns.

Card Meaning

The Knight of Pentacles is like the pizza delivery guy, always there when you need him. His offerings might seem mundane in the world of chivalry and romance, but they are dependable. You know that there will be no surprises and you will generally get exactly what you asked for. The Knight of Pentacles represents the element of fire in the suit of Earth. His passions will not burn out of control, rather they will tend to seem dull and not very visible. This card speaks to matters of money and finance, as there is a heavily materialistic side to this Knight.

When you draw this card in a reading, as with all the Knights, you are being asked to consider the direction that you are taking. Although it may seem boring, perhaps a more responsible attitude is called for, as in matters that involve saving rather than spending. The presence of this card tells you that nothing is going to be easily obtained, rather it will take hard work and perseverance. Since the Pentacle suit is concerned with physical comforts, the emotional side of things might be neglected in favor of material gain.

The shadow side of this card is the emotional detachment and overly materialistic emphasis on success. There is a tendency to be complacent and therefore take either people or situations for granted. This card is suggesting that you do not blunt your ability to be surprised by being overly methodical.

Kitchen Wisdom

Slow and steady wins the race, but it does not make for an exciting ride.

Queen of Pentacles

The Queen of Pentacles sits in her kitchen, surrounded by the signs of all her activity. Apple trees that she has planted and harvested form perfect rows outside the window. The fruit themselves line the windowsill and an apple pie is cooling on a nearby table. A loosely tied cloth bag lies beside her, its coins spilling out onto the brightly checkered tablecloth. She has found the time to dress herself in an elaborate and somewhat formal outfit with a crown perched jauntily on her head. She is well aware of her accomplishments, and is very secure in her role as the provider of all creature comforts. She spreads her arms wide as she welcomes you to sit down, have a cup of tea, and a chat.

Key Elements

Queen: All the Queens of the Tarot Court are associated with the water element. They are very knowledgeable about the emotional aspects of life, and deal with them in accordance to the nature of their suits. Pentacles contain heavy earth energy and represent the five senses, creature comforts, and financial undertakings. This queen is both sensuous and practical. She is a tribute to all working mothers as she provides both financial and domestic security.

Apples: Apple trees symbolize the feminine self. They are also emblems of magic, youth, and immortality. The apple itself is often associated with knowledge and temptation, and was a key player in the loss of innocence in the Garden of Eden. In this card, the apple is seen as fruit of the earth, a literal reminder of the abundance that is found in nature. The apple pie is a well-known symbol of hearth and home and signifies spiritual as well as physical contentment.

Bag of Coins: Money is obviously about wealth. It symbolizes financial success and sometimes greed. The bag in this card is not securely tied, meaning that the "purse strings" are easily opened and the material gifts are freely offered. The five coins relate to the five senses and the five points of a pentagram.

CARD MEANING

The Queen of Pentacles is water element in the suit of Earth. She represents fertility and abundance along with a well-grounded and practical sensibility. This Queen is able to combine material success with sensual pleasure and is known for being the essential "Earth Mother." Although she would be happiest working in the garden and tending to animals and children, she is very capable of maintaining a career and financial independence. This is the type of woman who brings home the bacon, and fries it in a pan. She can be a little intimidating to those less organized and competent.

When you draw this card in a reading, you are being asked to consider your feelings towards this kind of person. Do you feel empathetic towards her house-proud attitude and her ability to nurture those around her? Are you envious of her capability and success? Do you think she is wasting her time and energy at home, when she should be traveling or enjoying intellectual pursuits? Your reaction to this Queen is significant, because it points towards your current priorities. The Queen of Pentacles appears in a reading in order to remind you that it is important to nurture yourself as well as others.

The shadow side to this queen is twofold. It involves an overly materialistic attitude and a desire to control others by creating a co-dependency: giving too much instead of allowing others to do things for themselves. The differences between nurturing and smothering are often very subtle.

KITCHEN WISDOM

Add an "s" to mothering and you have smothering, which is only good when it comes to gravy.

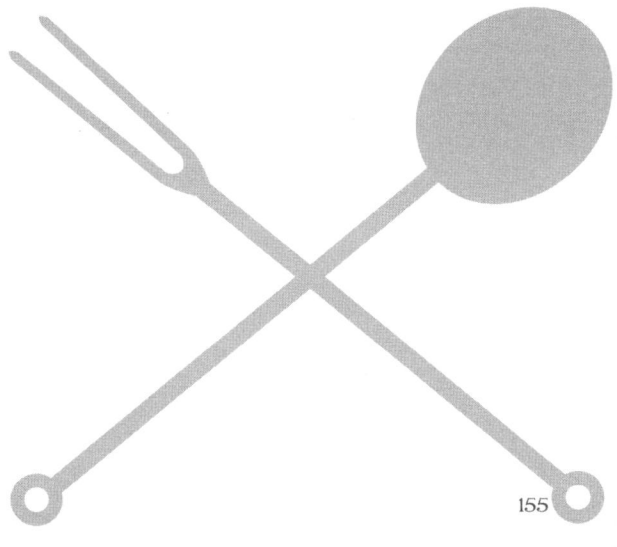

King of Pentacles

This King is very comfortable. The warmth of the fire, the snoring of his dog, and a full belly have lulled him to sleep. He is very casually dressed and does not look very regal, despite the large gold pentacle emblazoned on his T-shirt. There is a slice of apple pie and a glass of red wine waiting for him when he wakes up. It would seem that he has already eaten an apple, as just a core remains. The only thing that prevents this scene from being a template for domestic harmony and bliss is the woman hovering in the background. She is wearing an apron, and has her head bowed while she holds a crown on a platter. Is this the Queen who has baked the pie and now is humbly waiting for her husband to wake up and assume his kingly duties? Is she being quiet out of consideration, and does not want to disturb his brief moment of respite? Or is she afraid to wake him up because he will be angry and throw the apple core at her?

Key Elements

King: All Kings represent the power and success of their particular suits. They are also all associated with the element air, which allows them intellectual prowess and the ability to make decisions in a fair and rational manner. As Pentacles are an earth-based suit, the King of Pentacles is ruler of all earthly concerns. He centers his attention on family and home, but is equally successful in the world of finance. He has a reputation for being a kind and generous provider. He is known for his appreciation of the finer things in life, and loves children and animals.

Apple: Apples have long been associated with the suit of Pentacles, in great part because of the five-pointed star that is seen when an apple is cut in half horizontally. The number of seeds in the apple were used for divination purposes. Apples are also seen as symbols of longevity and prosperity. Conversely they can also be symbols of discord, as when a golden apple was thrown to Paris by the goddess Eris. It was supposed to be given to his choice of the most beautiful woman in the world. The Trojan Wars began after Paris handed the apple to Helen of Troy. The Adam's apple in a man is supposed to mark the spot where the apple from the Garden of Eden stuck in Adam's throat, after he took a bite. It symbolizes the fall of man. The apple core is, in part, tribute to the goddess Kore, closely associated with the rituals surrounding the pentagram, and to the phrase, "getting to the core of the matter." Peel back the layers in order to get to the real issues at hand.

Card Meaning

The King of Pentacles is shown resting in a large comfortable chair, with his eyes closed and a smile on his face. He is the personification of domestic contentment. He is the only King to be shown with closed eyes. This is because he is the most sensuous of them all. He indulges his physical needs and also is secure in the knowledge that he is safe and will remain undisturbed.

The woman waiting patiently in the background, holding his crown, knows this. She does not appear to be resentful, although her head is bowed in a subservient manner.

The King of Pentacles is about being king of one's castle. He takes a possessive view towards all his belongings and that often includes members of his household. He is a hard-working man who, at the end of the day, would rather be home than anywhere else. Like the rest of the Pentacle Court, he is conservative in his thinking, painstaking in his actions, and very concerned with financial security.

When you draw this card in a reading, you are being asked to describe who the King sees when he opens his eyes and looks at the woman standing there. Your interpretation of the situation will tell you your relationship to this card. If you see an equal and considerate partner, you are in a position to be generous to others who might need your help or support. If you see a maid or stranger, then you are the one who will be needing to seek out the King for your own welfare.

The shadow side to this King is that he can be overly indulgent with his appetites, which include, sex, food, alcohol, and money. On a bad day, he can be domineering and controlling with little patience for the opinion of others.

Kitchen Wisdom

The King exists because others need him to.

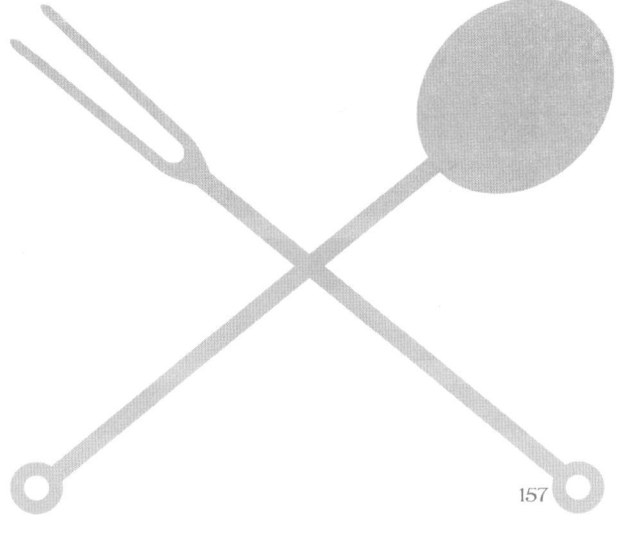

CONCLUSION

This deck was created out of a desire to understand the Tarot. I can honestly say that I will never stop discovering new elements of this timeless craft. I would personally like to see Tarot become an acknowledged part of the healthcare system. Self-awareness and an understanding of our desires and motivations go a long way towards promoting good mental health.

Thank you for coming on this journey with me,
and may all your kitchens be blessed.